Typography Primer

by Anthony Faiola

GATFPress
Pittsburgh

International Standard Book Number: 0-88362-262-9
Library of Congress Catalog Card Number: 00-101668

Printed in the United States of America
Catalog No. 1705
First Edition
July 2000

GATF*Press* books are widely used by companies, associations, and schools
for training, marketing, and resale. Quantity discounts are available by
contacting Peter Oresick at 800/910-GATF.

GATF*Press*   **Orders to:**
Graphic Arts Technical Foundation   GATF Orders
200 Deer Run Road   P.O. Box 1020
Sewickley, PA 15143-2600   Sewickley, PA 15143-1020
Phone: 412/741-6860   Phone (U.S. and Canada): 800/662-3916
Fax: 412/741-2311   Phone (all other countries): 412/741-5733
Email: info@gatf.org   Fax: 412/741-0609
Internet: http://www.gatf.org   Email: gatforders@abdintl.com

TABLE OF CONTENTS

Dedicated to Lynda

FOREWORD

A crash course in typography? Yes, that's what we have asked of Anthony Faiola, assistant professor in the Department of Computer Graphics in the area of interactive media development in the School of Technology at Purdue University. This book offers a short, non-technical orientation to the field.

The aim of the GATF*Press* primer series is to communicate the essential concepts of printing processes and technologies. Other primers focus on computer-to-plate, lithography, flexography, gravure, on-demand, digital, and screen printing, and new titles are being planned.

Typography Primer is useful to students, graphic artists, print buyers, publishers, salespeople in the graphic communications industry—to anyone who would like to know more about the printing process.

GATF*Press* is committed to serving the graphic communications community as a leading publisher of technical information. Please visit the GATF website at http://www.gatf.org for additional information about our resources and services.

Peter Oresick
Director
GATF*Press*

PREFACE

This book is intended for the growing population of both novices and young professionals in the areas of visual communication, graphic arts, technical communications/journalism, and multimedia design. Although this book focuses primarily on the theoretical aspects of typography, it does provide some application of the concepts. This book is a tool for beginners who desire to understand the historic, mechanical, and visual science of typography. It is not a design book per se, but rather a guide to inform the user of a basic knowledge of typography.

In this basic text on typography, I have attempted to provide type from a historical perspective first. Knowing the historical development of typography can provide an appreciation of letterforms. Second, by understanding the visual science of type, a beginner can cultivate more than an aesthetic reference to evaluating the use of type. Typography is not only about the beauty of letterforms but also the deliberate science of communication that allows cultures, nations, and communities to communicate effectively.

In aspects of legibility and readability of type, studies show that concern for the visual science of typography substantially adds to the value of any graphic product. Graphic technologists who design new media products are becoming increasingly concerned with a range of visual-based problems that extend beyond the mere aesthetic. As a result, visual language and the use of any typographic system should involve an aesthetic, as well as scientific, means to more accurately evaluate the effective response from user interaction. This is why digital typographers and designers have more recently expressed the need to measure the legibility of type in order to better gauge the reader's ability to quickly and smoothly find, identify, discriminate, and obtain the information relevant to their needs. In an age of information overload, this is becoming the conventional wisdom of design professionals who use type and other forms of visual language systems to effectively communicate information.

Today the principles of typography, whether delivered on paper or digital display, are still independent of the delivery medium. The most significant difference, however, is the fact that when we consider the World Wide Web and other forms of new media, we must design in such a way that the result will be "attractively effective." In other words, it provides optimum visual appeal and clarity, regardless of the user's choice of operating system, browser, monitor size, or any of the many variables available. Of course, this makes designing for the Web a more challenging enterprise than for print, especially because of the dimension of navigation. Nevertheless, the laws of visual language must still play a dominant role in the design and use of type, as demonstrated by the great typographers of the past six centuries.

ACKNOWLEDGMENTS

Special thanks to my assistant Doug Sutton for helping me collect much of the background material for this text.

I also would like to thank GATF's Peter Oresick and his students at Carnegie Mellon University for the editorial services they contributed to this project as a part of the course "Publishing in the Information Age" during the Spring 2000 semester.

Warit Achavanuntakul
Eva Bai
Andy Butts
Nalini Garg
Aaron Goldstein
Uday Gupta
Stacey Jenkins
Marcin Jeske
Saurin Jhaveri
Karen Loong
Sheel Mohnot
Seth Mandel
Reiko Medina
Che Fung So
Lee-Anne Stussell
Nitya Venkataraman
Mika Yasuoka

1 A BRIEF HISTORY OF TYPOGRAPHY

INTRODUCTION

For as long as humans have existed, evidence shows they have made images recording aspects of their daily lives. During these early stages of image-making, about 30,000 to 4000 B.C., their ability to recall concepts and events was supported by the images they could generate on demand. These early graphic forms of communication represent the first attempts of a system of visual-based language.

Although primitive, cave drawings and carvings on bones or stones were used to represent human experience before the development of agriculture (Figure 1-1). People of this period were from a hunting and gathering culture. The cave painting of a horse in Figure 1-2 is one of many that perfectly depict the level of detail exhibited by early cultures.

These early forms of visual language were not art as we might understand but rather a system of pictographs, ideographs, and ornamental images that also served a utilitarian function. Some historians believe that cave paintings had a variety of purposes—whether to serve as a teaching

Figure 1-1. One of the first accepted pieces of prehistoric art is the Venus of Willendorf, made of limestone and dating to c. 30,0000–25,000 B.C.

manual to prepare their youth in the art of stalking their prey, as instructions on the rites of a spiritual ceremony, or in honor of the hunt.

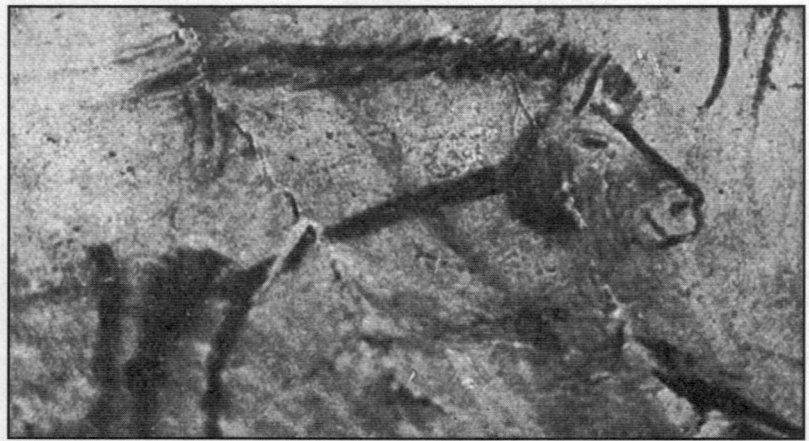

Figure 1-2. Detail of early cave rendering.

ANCIENT WRITING SYSTEMS

By 4000 B.C. humans transformed from a nomadic lifestyle to a loosely formed community of cave dwellers. Such groups eventually developed into a higher form of civilization in the Fertile Crescent of Mesopotamia. Their visual language reflected their progress intellectually, socially, economically, spiritually, culturally, govern-mentally, agriculturally, and technologically. The exactitude with which humans portrayed their daily experience in stylized symbols matched the progress of their spoken language.

During this time the Sumerian people, who settled in the land between the Euphrates and Tigris Rivers in Mesopotamia, devel-oped a system of worship with a variety of symbols that express the earliest recorded form of religion. The symbols of this period began to represent both physical objects and abstract concepts not visible to the eye. For example, the symbols of objects such as man, sun, moon, and water; concepts such as day, year, joy, and hate; or activities like walking, fighting, and worship are found throughout their written records.

By 2000–1800 B.C., the use of markings, clay seals, and trademarks began—and have continued through our present-day use in commercial products. At the same time a variety of methods of written communication had reached Egypt. The Egyptians are best known for their hieroglyphics, another form of pictograph (Figure 1-3). This form of picture writing goes back as far as 4000 B.C. until A.D. 400. The legacy of Egyptian hieroglyphics and illustrations still resonates throughout the pages of history along with the early development of Mesopotamian pictographs.

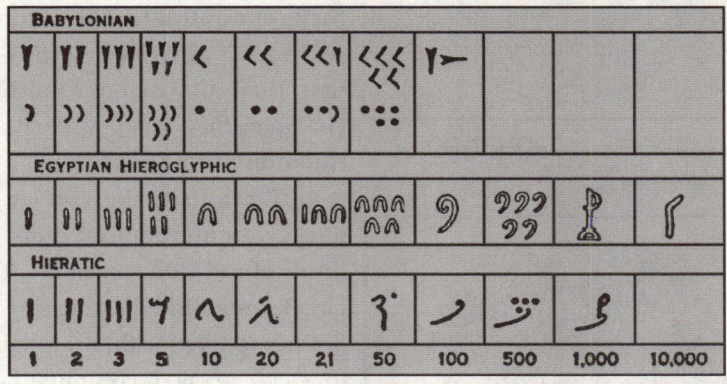

Figure 1-3. Early written language showing progression of the numbering system from Babylonian to Egyptian hieroglyphics to the hieratic forms.

Historians assert that an evolution of word symbols is clearly evident from Egyptian hieroglyphics (Figure 1-4) to the earliest alphabet of the Cretan and Phoenician visual language systems in 1000 B.C.

This new form of communication assigned specific sounds to each character, which gradually evolved into forming the first Greek letterforms by 700 B.C. One factor that highly contributed to the deciphering of hieroglyphics was the discovery of the Rosetta Stone by Jean Francois Champollion in 1822. The Rosetta Stone

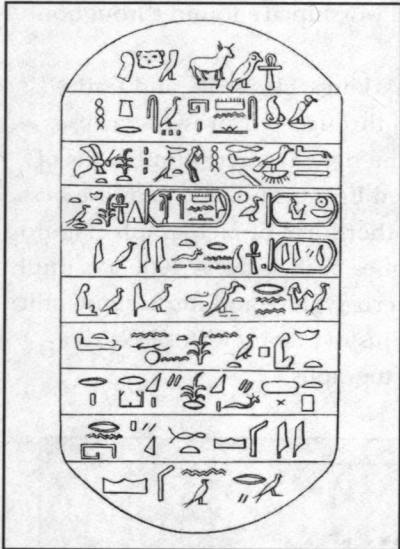

Figure 1-4. Example of late Egyptian hieroglyphics.

Figure 1-5. Papyrus plant growing in its natural swamp habitat.

dates back to 196 B.C. and has parallel inscriptions in hieroglyphics, the demotic system, and Greek letters that provided a key breakthrough to understanding Egyptian hieroglyphics.

Hieroglyphics led to innovative ways of recording information, such as the extensive use of papyrus, which was first developed by the Egyptians. Although the Greeks established the groundwork for the accomplishments of Western civilization, their alphabet dynamically changed the course of visual communication forever.

Previous pictograph language systems required hundreds of individual symbols. The Greeks established the use of limited letters for their alphabet in a wide array of combinations. This provided almost endless possibilities for forming new words or sounds.

By 300 B.C. the conquests of Alexander the Great helped to establish Greek as the common language spoken in most places controlled by Rome until A.D. 450. With Greek being used for official government business, Latin became the common language of the Roman citizen.

Values	Hieroglyphic	Hieratic.	Phœnician	Greek	Roman	Hebrew	
a	eagle			A	A	א	1
b	crane			B	B	ב	2
ḳ (g)	throne			Γ	C	ג	3
ṭ (d)	hand			Δ	D	ד	4
h	mæander			E	E	ה	5
f	cerastes			Y	F	ו	6
z	duck			I	Z	ז	7
χ (kh)	sieve			H	H	ח	8
θ (th)	tongs			Θ	...	ט	9
i	parallels			I	I	י	10
k	bowl			K	K	כ	11
l	lioness			Λ	L	ל	12
m	owl			M	M	מ	13
n	water			N	N	נ	14
s	chairback			Ξ	X	ס	15
å	....			O	O	ע	16
p	shutter			Π	P	פ	17
t' (ts)	snake			...	...	צ	18
q	angle			...	Q	ק	19
r	mouth			P	R	ר	20
š (sh)	inundated garden			Σ	S	ש	21
t	lasso			T	T	ת	22

Figure 1-6. Chart showing semantic evolution of visual language from Egyptian to Phoenician to Greek to Roman. Hebrew developed earlier, around 2000 B.C.

ABCDEFG
HIJKLMN
OPQRST
UVWXYZ
1234567890
abcdefghijklm
nopqrstuvwxyz

Figure 1-7. Early Roman characters.

Figure 1-8. Roman insignia showing Roman characters in all uppercase letters and the use of bullets or dots to separate letters.

Latin, with its Roman characters, was the first language to use serifs, and the Roman use of all capitals was one of several design styles beginning in the second century A.D.

The Roman alphabet, consisting of twenty-one letters, was the earliest manifestation of the English alphabet.

Writing materials such as parchment and papyrus were expensive, so the all-capitals letterform was used in a condensed style to conserve space. To maintain individual word clarity, a small bullet was used instead of space to separate words (Figure 1-8). The concept of conserving space was also introduced when the first century scribes transcribed the Greek manuscripts of the New Testament by removing the spaces between words (Figure 1-9).

During this time the codex was first used, as opposed to the previous use of scrolls. The codex was the first form of book as we know it today, i.e., with folded pages, with a left-and-right page format. The earliest practical form of book was made of

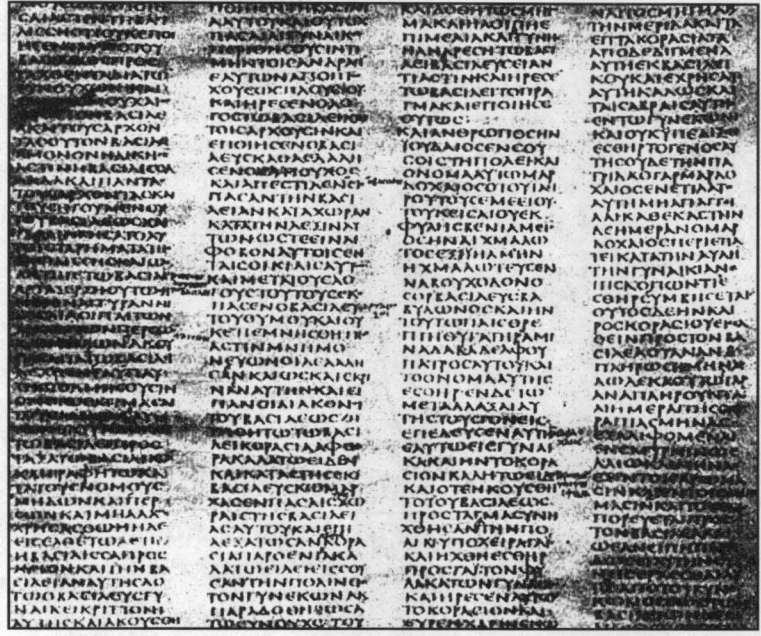

Figure 1-9. Early Greek text of New Testament written on papyrus paper that leaves no space between words or paragraphs to conserve space.

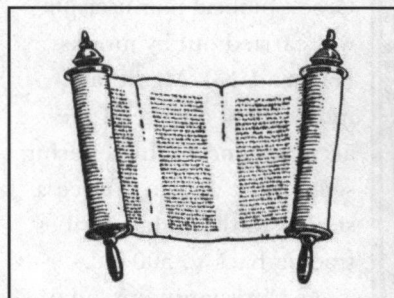

Figure 1-10. Early papyrus scroll used for religious and secular manuscripts. Pieces of papyrus were attached together and wound onto a roll. As the reader passed through the material, the scroll was rolled up on the left and unrolled on the right.

Figure 1-11. The earliest form of a book, called a codex, was made up of square sheets of papyrus or parchment that were written on and folded.

Figure 1-12. Early Greek scribe whose job was to accurately copy text from one manuscript to another.

Figure 1-13. Medieval monks were employed to transcribe manuscripts, the Bible, and music, as illustrated here.

parchment which could be folded in two and bound together by stitching.

By A.D. 395, fifty-five years after Constantine had become the Roman Emperor, the Roman Empire was divided and eventually overrun by Germanic Barbarians. This gradually affected the language of the people, as well as the look of their written communication.

MIDDLE AGES TYPOGRAPHY

From A.D. 400 to 600 the responsibility of copying all of the ancient Latin and Greek biblical manuscripts was carried out by monks (Figure 1-13). Medieval monks kept charge of the accuracy and of the lettering style of the copying process, similar to the Judaic scribes tracing back to 500 B.C.

As Christianity spread north into Ireland, the Celtic lettering style brought another unique form of design to the transcription of religious manuscripts. By A.D. 600 to 900 Celtic letterforms

Figure 1-14. Celtic alphabet.

(Figure 1-14) included four significant aspects. First, their letterforms possessed more rounded uncials that demonstrated the first clear resemblance to our present-day uppercase and lowercase text. Second, these upper- and lowercase letters increased readability and saved space. Third, the Celtics' innovation of word space was introduced, which also contributed most notably to the overall readability of text. And fourth, the Celtic manuscript decorations and capital letters had a special geometric ornamentation.

Figure 1-15. Celtic letter B.

Figure 1-16. Romanesque letter P.

ABCD'OEEFGhJBLM
MNOPQRSGUVXYZ

Figure 1-17. Romanesque alphabet.

From A.D. 900 to 1000, the Carolinian style of lettering was introduced as the standard for copying all ancient manuscripts. And by the end of the first millennium, the Romanesque lettering style evolved from the Carolinian style (Figure 1-17). This included letters that were combined, inset, or extremely reshaped to form new characters.

By A.D. 1200, the Romanesque style had further evolved into a more Gothic look, which is referred to as the Black Letter type style, commonly referred to as Old English. By the late Gothic to early Renaissance periods (A.D. 1300 to the 1500s), Black Letter had become the copying standard throughout Europe, both for religious and secular manuscripts.

RENAISSANCE TYPOGRAPHY

In A.D. 1438, as the men of the Renaissance reflected upon the profound meaning of the universe, the first printed Bibles of Johann Gutenberg (Figures 1-18 and 1-19) were being made available to the multitudes throughout Germany.

Within ten years print shops and book fairs spread throughout Europe. The age-old process of writing out an entire book by hand was tedious and labor-intensive, but Gutenberg's innovation was a revolution in Western com-

Figure 1-18. Johann Gutenberg.

Figure 1-19. A page from Gutenberg's forty-two-line Bible.

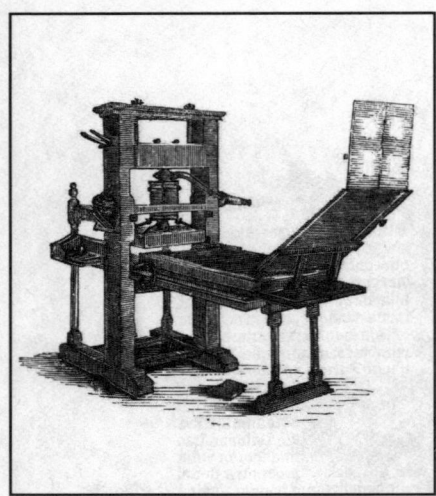

Figure 1-20. Example of Gutenberg's first printing press.

Figure 1-21. Typical fifteenth century print shop. Men ink the text block with inking dabbers where they will lay the paper for printing.

munication systems. This was because individual Latin letters of cast lead could now be reused—a technique referred to as movable type. Each letter was modeled and cut by hand from hard metal to form a punch. This basic technology of hot metal casting was used quite heavily right up until the 1960s.

Gutenberg used Black Letter for his first letter castings because this was the common handwritten letterform of the day. Peter Schoeffer designed the font under Gutenberg's supervision. The font was a very accurate imitation of the best style of the period, and it contained nearly three hundred letters, ligatures, and abbreviations.

Printers eventually found that people generally preferred the more Roman style of Rotunda because its letterform was more rounded and easier to read. By the 1450s the Black Letter typeface was abandoned for the Roman Old Style typeface called Cloister Old Style, invented by Frenchman Nicholas Jenson. This Roman-style font is one of the greatest typefaces ever designed because of its sheer beauty and the precision with which Jenson chiseled every character.

Giovanbattista Palatino, also known as the "calligrapher's calligrapher," designed twenty-nine different scripts and also designed Latin, German, Hebrew, Chaldee, Arabic, Greek, Egyptian, Syrian, Indian, Cyrillic (Russian), and several other alphabets.

By 1494 Aldus Manutius, an Italian printer and scholar from Venice, created the first modern book on the graphic design of typography. It focused on the legibility of print, the care of the letter stroke, and the use of serifs. In 1501 Manutius employed typographer Francesco Griffo da Bologna to cut his famous Italic typefaces. In Venice this type was known as "Aldino" or "Venetian," but in Germany and the Netherlands it was called "cursive," and in France it was called "Italian" or "Italic."

At about this time Francesco Griffo also designed the Bembo typeface, which became a subject of study for many artists throughout Europe well into the sixteenth century. Claude Garamond's

Roman typeface, designed in 1530, is one of the best-known letterform designs in history. Its slick, well-engineered form allows each letter to fit well, side by side, with geometric precision and elegance.

SEVENTEENTH CENTURY TO MODERN TYPOGRAPHY

Figure 1-22. Typical eighteenth century print shop. Men still use the ink-dabbing technique; the use of inking rollers was not introduced until the industrial revolution during the middle to late nineteenth century.

Upon entering the seventeenth century, typographers estab-

Figure 1-23. Portrait of William Caslon.

Figure 1-24. Portrait of John Baskerville.

Figure 1-25. Portrait of Giambattisa Bodoni.

lished both geometric formulas and measuring systems for letterform design. A whole new use of type began to be used as well. From the late 1600s to the late 1800s, the printing press and typecasting technology had very limited developments, but the rise of the industrial age brought quick change.

Soon after the first printing company opened in the United States in 1640, a number of shops opened all over the thirteen colonies. At this point a reliable international system of typographical measurement had yet to be formed. In the earlier days of printing, different sizes of type had simply been called by different names. "Brevier" was simply the British name for 8-point type of any style; 8-point type was called "Petit Texte" by the French and "Testino" by the Italians.

In 1737 Pierre Fournier, a Frenchman, published his book, *Table of Proportions*, which assigned a comprehensive system of select sizes to type. We still use Fournier's system of points and picas in the computer desktop publishing systems of today. Fournier's book was later refined by Francois Ambroise Didot, which assigned approximately 72 points to the inch, establishing the "point" measuring system for type. By this time typestyles were no longer designed merely for books but for use in newspapers, pamphlets, fliers, and an assortment of other printed matter for business and personal use.

In Europe, from the early to late 1800s, typographers like William Caslon, John Baskerville, Giambattisa Bodoni, and Didot designed the typefaces which are still commonly used today. And in the nineteenth century, Caslon's Caslon IV sans serif typeface began a trend that is still with us today.

With the birth of the industrial revolution, advertising became the unique way for the modern world to market its products, and sans serif type established its place in advertising. A large variety of sans serif display faces for headlines, posters, and billboards began to be used. No longer was type merely a vehicle for common use in literature or higher books of learning, but now typography joined the ranks of commercialism as a new form of communication that would spread throughout the world. From 1880 to World War I, the late Victorian period was characterized by its ornamental style of art and type, having an asymmetrical and flowing delicacy of form.

TWENTIETH CENTURY TYPOGRAPHY

The twentieth century brought even more uses for type. In this century, typographers such as Rudolf Koch and Frederic Goudy began to design letterforms reminiscent of the Medieval and Renaissance periods. The Dada and avant-garde artists Marcel Duchamp, El Lissitzky, and those of the Bauhaus and Constructivist movements also did exploration into type as art. Their work reflected the influence of the mechanical exactness of the industrial age.

Appearing in the 1920s and 1930s, the Art Nouveau, or "new art," movement introduced a similarly distinctive style to typography. Likewise, Art Deco captured beauty in geometric simplicity and its distinctive sans serif letterform. By 1927 Paul Renner had designed his graceful geometric sans serif Futura typeface, and Jan Tschichold wrote *The New Typographer,* a book on type design, page layout, and grid systems.

As a precursor to phototypesetting in the 1960s, the first photocomposition device was introduced in 1944. This machine, developed by Frenchmen Louis Moyroud and René Higonnet, was referred to as the "Photon." Harris Intertype's Fotosetter, an adaptation of a linecasting machine, made its debut in 1949. By the

Figure 1-26. Marcel Duchamp's famous painting, Bride Descending a Staircase, demonstrates the mechanical influence of the industrial age on art and type.

1960s, setting type had changed from hot type set in lead to cold type set photographically. This technology was called phototypesetting, by which a negative containing all of the characters of a single font or font family was exposed by light through which a clear, crisp type image was transferred to photosensitive paper. In this process, type could be enlarged and manipulated in a number of new ways, such as extending, condensing, bending, angling, and distorting. This allowed typographers to experiment easily with word, sentence, and line spacing.

Also from the 1960s to 1980s there was a revival in Art Nouveau, Art Deco, and many Old-Style typefaces. Typographers redesigned these historic typefaces with a new zeal, while maintaining the modern influences of proportion. Much can be said about the desktop publishing and digital design revolution of the 1980s, for which Apple Computer takes chief responsibility. This decade ushered in the greatest flood of new typefaces. The desktop computer now provided the masses the way to explore typography in ways that are still spilling over into the typographic forms of this century.

The 1990s also ushered in a new movement in typography referred to as Trash or Fringe type, which tells a story beyond the words. Some call it "grunge typography" from the rock music movement. Some critics consider it a merger of the industrial functionalist movement with the wild, nihilistic absurdity of Dadaism. Nevertheless, these typefaces express, in part, the design culture of the age, just as all the previous typographic letterforms portrayed the attitude of their times.

2 THE EVOLUTION OF TYPOGRAPHIC STYLES

INTRODUCTION

Most typographers, graphic designers, and graphic arts professionals classify typefaces by categories called "races" or "species." Within
these species there are subsets of families of type, which exhibit
their own personal design characteristics. These characteristics
together form a particular trait profile that make it special and
more preferable than others. For practical clarity it is easier to dis-
cuss type from the perspective of having a family classification or
category.

Once a typeface category is understood in terms of legibility
and suitability, the selection of a typeface becomes a problem-free
process. Whether a graphics professional is selecting a typeface for
a particular design project or purchasing it for a digital library,
these categories provide an easy system by which to understand
and apply type.

There is still some debate as to the classification in which some
typefaces belong and how many classifications there are. The
author has, however, attempted to follow the general rule of eight
classifications plus one. For the sake of clarity, this additional category is Trash Type, which has been added to simplify the broad
range of different twentieth century stylized fonts that do not fit
into the conventional classifications. These classifications are
(1) Black Letter, (2) Roman, (3) Sans Serif, (4) Square Serif,
(5) Script/Cursive, (6) Italic, (7) Decorative/Novelty, (8) Glyphic,
and (9) Trash Type.

BLACK LETTER

Black Letter, also known as Textura, Text, or Old English, resembles calligraphy or handwritten script. Originally Black Letter was drawn by German scribes dating from A.D. 300 to the 1400s. Black Letter dominated northern Europe throughout the medieval age. About 1435 Peter Shoeffer was employed by Gutenberg to design and cast the first Black Letter typeface for his forty-two-line Mainz Bible.

Black Letter is considered one of the most ornate typefaces, featuring a great variation in strokes within each character. Black Letter is sometimes referred to as **Textura** because from a distance a full page resembles a piece of woven cloth. Today Black Letter is most often used for printed materials related to traditional occasions such as weddings, graduations, religious events, and official documents intended to reflect the feeling of the Medieval period.

Figure 2-1. Examples of Black Letter typefaces.

ROMAN

From the beginning of the Renaissance period, southern Europeans preferred the simpler, lighter, and more delicate letterforms of the Romans, which replaced the heavy, ornate look of Black Letter. This was based primarily on their aesthetic preferences and principles of readability. The Roman category of letterform was developed in Venice, Paris, and elsewhere throughout southern Europe. As discussed previously, the Romans adapted their alphabet from the ancient Greeks, an alphabet that can be traced back to the hieroglyphics of the Egyptians.

The distinguishing historical feature of the Roman race of type is the serif. The ancient Roman inscriber used a brush to make curves and continuous lines to write inscriptions on their buildings. All Roman type has serifs and letter strokes that vary in width from thick to thin. The inscriber finished each character with a long, broad arrow by using the side of the brush, which produced the serifs on each letter. The three letterform attributes that contribute to the special appearance of a Roman character to differentiate its appearance from other typefaces are (1) serifs, (2) light and heavy strokes, and (3) curved width.

The serifs found on the bottom of letters rest on the horizontal baseline, helping to tie the letters together to form words. The top serifs contribute to the unique appearance of the letter and help readability.

The serifs on the lowercase letters slant and are bracketed; that is, they connect to the main strokes with a curve, making a gentle transition from thick to thin.

Other special characteristics of Roman letterforms are: (1) the ascenders and descenders, which further assist in the font identification and word recognition, and (2) that by drawing a line through the thinnest parts of the rounded letters, the diagonal line exhibits what is called the "diagonal stress" of the typeface.

The Roman typefaces are the most widely used and are by far the greatest in number. Roman type is classified in three groups according to chronological development: **Old Style, Transitional,** and **Modern.**

Old Style

Old Style typefaces are characterized by three distinct attributes:
(1) limited contrast between the thick and thin stroke lines,
(2) strokes that are sloping or round, or (3) serifs that are slanted

Bookman Old Style
Garamond
Palatino
Times Roman
Weiss

Figure 2-2. Examples of Old Style typefaces.

Americana
Baskerville
New Century Schoolbook
Times New Roman

Figure 2-3. Examples of Transitional typefaces.

Bauer Bodoni
Bodoni
New Caledonia Roman
Walbaum

Figure 2-4. Examples of Modern typefaces.

or curved and extend outward, e.g., at the top of the capital *T* and the bottom of the capital *E*.

Old Style Roman typefaces generally have a warm, graceful appearance, providing the best choice for setting lengthy bodies of text. Old Style Roman makes words more readable for a smooth, uninterrupted flow as the eye moves across the words.

The first Roman letterforms by Nicholas Jenson were inspired by ancient Roman characters found on monuments that utilized all capital letters. Jenson, however, followed the tradition of the scribes by using lowercase letters. As a result, each word could be viewed separately, having its own shape and identity.

TRANSITIONAL

Transitional Roman typefaces are often overlooked by many designers as an important style. Transitional typefaces appeared during a brief period in typographic history and should include letterforms that fall between the Old Style typeface (with sloping/rounded strokes, little contrast between thick and thin lines, slanting or curved serifs) and the Modern typeface (with contrasting thick and thin strokes and unbracketed serifs). Also, the lowercase characters are shorter than the Old Style characters. John Baskerville's improvement on the **Caslon** typeface is one good example, as well as his **Baskerville** typeface, the first typeface used to print on smooth paper.

MODERN

An Italian type designer named Giambattista Bodoni introduced the so-called Modern Roman typefaces in 1773. Modern typefaces have elegance yet tend to have a more rigid appearance than Old Style typefaces. Modern type reflects an emphasis on structure and form, with little reminiscence of its roots tracing back to handwritten letterforms. Modern Roman attributes have six distinct characteristics: (1) a strong contrast between thick and thin strokes, (2) little or no bracketing, (3) no cursive where the serif meets the stroke, (4) a radical change from thick to thin where the strokes

Arial
Avant Garde
Eurostile
Futura
Helvetica
Univers 55 Regular

Figure 2-5. Examples of Sans Serif typefaces.

American Typewriter
Glypha
Lubalin Graph
Memphis
Serifa
Rockwell

Figure 2-6. Examples of Square Serif typefaces.

create the letterform, (5) a stress that is not absolutely vertical, and (6) long ascenders and descenders.

By the late eighteenth century, Modern typefaces reflected a thinner look and lines became much sharper, while the overall quality and aesthetic form began to decline. **Bodoni** is one of the most famous typefaces of this period.

SANS SERIF

Although Sans Serif typefaces have some ancient derivatives, it is comparatively new. Most of the similarities are from the flat, even-bodied lines of the Greek and early Roman letters. The word *sans* is derived from the French word meaning "without"; that is, they are typefaces without serifs. Some typographers refer to them as being monotonal. Being one of the newest type species of the twentieth century, sans serifs are still an all-purpose font that exhibits an excellent graphic impact in all types of designs.

Sans Serif typefaces are generally formed with strokes of uniform width, are geometric in form, are precise and open, and tend to have very large x-heights.

The Sans Serifs became especially popular in the 1920s when the Bauhaus movement in Germany made its impact in the world of typography. The concern of the Bauhaus designers for the functionality of typography caused them to use type that reduced the letterform to its essential form, which is epitomized in the **Futura** typeface. Sans Serif fonts are used more and more, especially in logo design, newsletters, and in-house publications.

SQUARE SERIF

Square Serifs have the general characteristics of Sans Serifs except that a square straight-line serif is added. Some typographers refer to the Square Serif as the Slab Serif because of this feature. It also has been referred to as the Egyptian Serif because in the early nineteenth century there was great interest in the 1799 discovery of the Rosetta Stone in Egypt.

Square Serif typefaces are usually formed with strokes of equal width, like Sans Serif typefaces, but have finishing-off strokes added. The shape of the serif is square or block-like, and the serif has the same width as the main portion of the letter face. They reflect the sturdy, square look of steel girders, giving the reader the feeling of strength, stability, and ruggedness. Seldom should Square Serif typefaces be used for straight body copy on a page because it is not as easy to read as type with thinner serifs.

Square Serifs are best used as a display font for headlines, headings in advertisements, and posters. There are many forms of Square Serif typefaces, many with Egyptian family names or with names that are descriptive of the type style they portray.

SCRIPT AND CURSIVE

Script and Cursive styles clearly reflect their names; that is, they resemble handwriting. The similarity of Script and Cursive letterforms caused the author to categorize them together. Clarification should be made, however, in the difference between Script and Cursive type styles. Some typographers have strictly defined Script styles as those that have connecting letters and Cursive styles as having letters that are separated with a slight gap. At the same time some say the complete opposite.

The purpose and function of both Script and Cursive typefaces are to simulate handwriting and to generate a particular feeling throughout a design. Script and Cursive typefaces express a special touch that evoke delicacy, elegance, and the spice of life when used for invitations, announcements, diplomas, or other pieces for special occasions.

When Script and Cursive type styles are used extensively throughout a document, low readability levels will be incurred, as they put a great strain on the reader. As with Black Letter typefaces, Script and Cursive typefaces should be avoided when text length is more than a focused line or group of sentences.

Kaufmann Script

Mistral

Park Avenue

Zapf Chancery

Figure 2-7. Examples of Script and Cursive typefaces.

ITALIC

Although Aldus Manutius developed the first Italic typeface in the 1490s, many designers of his time considered it to be a cursive letter style because it possessed the free-flowing handwriting characteristic of his time. Actually, its name comes from the Latin word *curare,* which means "to run."

Italic type is often used to emphasize a specific body of copy, while adding a special flare to the text. Practical applications include Italic typefaces that indicate specialty in the text. For example, poetry is often seen in an Italic face. It is also used for book or article titles, foreign words, special terms, and for quotations.

Although most Roman faces have companion Italics, it is not a slanted version of the upright Roman letterform. Merely slanting fonts, whether they are serifed or sans serifed type styles, should be considered by name as an Oblique typeface. Obliquing the letterform of text can only produce a limited emulation of an Italic font and does not constitute a true italicizing. Obliquing can be done

Times New Roman Italic

Bodoni Italic

Figure 2-8. Examples of Italic typefaces.

Bauhaus 93

DESDEMONA

Braggadocio

Korinna

Bernhard

Hobo

STENCIL

Figure 2-9. Examples of Decorative and Novelty typefaces.

COPPERPLATE

Friz Quadrata Roman

Poppl-Laudatio Regular

Serif Gothic

Figure 2-10. Examples of Glyphic typefaces.

easily with any desktop publishing system and will be discussed in more detail later in this volume.

DECORATIVE AND NOVELTY

It has always been challenging to identify the broad category of Decorative and Novelty within the bounds of a single font family. The earliest Decorative and Novelty typefaces appeared during the Art Deco movement in the early twentieth century and continue to have great appeal for many designers today.

This classification is used for a wide variety of typefaces whose primary intent is to create special attention and add whimsy and fun to design. Unfortunately, Decorative and Novelty typefaces are obscure and put readability at an impossible level. Without exception, they are almost always used as display type for headings or subheadings. Generally, the same kinds of graphic laws apply to Decorative and Novelty typefaces that apply to Script and Cursive typefaces. That is, they must be carefully chosen to give a specific appearance or generate a special mood in the designed copy, but they should not be used for lengthy body copy of any kind.

GLYPHIC

This category simply defies the previous formal classifications, yet these typefaces are also commonly used today. They are a special breed of type with expressed traits that appear to be constructed in a special contemporary style, rather than the more formal Roman typefaces used for extensive reading text. Some typographers classify this typeface category as Glyphic, while others prefer to keep it in the Decorative category. Although some of these typefaces are viable contenders for use in larger bodies of text, they often are used in all caps as display type.

The appearance of Glyphic typefaces are based on letterforms that have been chiseled out of stone, rather than drawn with the traditional pen or brush. This is especially noticeable with the chiseled look of the stroke endings and the triangle-shaped serifs.

TRASH TYPE

Trash, also referred to as Fringe or Grunge Type, pushes the boundaries of aesthetics far more than Decorative or Novelty. It can be wacky, silly, very distorted, trashy, and, above all, on the far fringes of what is traditionally accepted as real type—and it is almost impossible to read. With a good sense of humor, you have to see the simple beauty in their sheer ugliness and unreadability. As with all Trash type, it differs from the typographic styles of the past because it is not only a revolution in typographic style but also a rebellion to the principles of legibility.

Since digital typography hit its stride in the 1980s, font creation software has put the power of type design into the hands of many who otherwise would never consider themselves qualified to try their hand at the art of letterforms. With the power to create personal typefaces, all the rules of traditional design and typography have been blurred. As we entered into the 1990s, the conservative

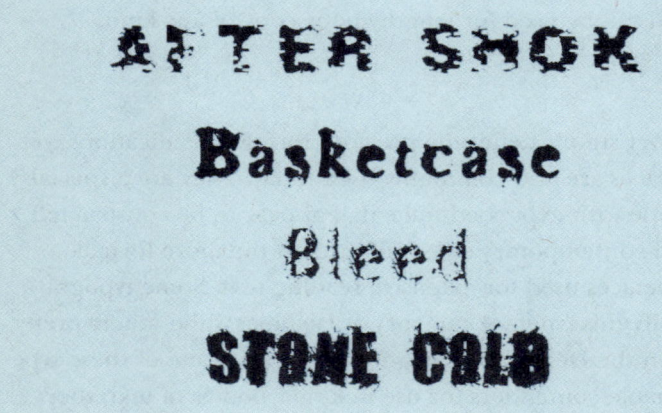

Figure 2-11. Examples of Trash Type typefaces.

guidelines of type design began to disintegrate to make room for a new generation of typographers, designers, and a wide variety of graphic technologists.

In the twenty-first century, the age-old art of typography is still evolving. As long as societies and their culture of communications evolve, new forms of typography will supply the need to communicate the visual language that best matches the culture of the times.

3 TYPOGRAPHY BASICS

INTRODUCTION

TYPEFACE NAMES OF THE PAST

Today it is common to refer to a typeface by name and then separately refer to its point size by number. Before 1737, however, a typeface name referred to its type size; i.e., the point size of a particular typeface was identified by name not by number. For example, 10-point type was called Long Primer, 18-point was called Greater Primer, and 36-point was called Double Great Primer. As the old system of specification ceased, typefaces took on the name of their creator or style rather than size as identification. Some typefaces that took on the names of their creators are Bodoni, Baskerville, and Garamond, and some typefaces that took on the names of their styles or other forms are Times Roman, Helvetica, and Rockwell.

WHAT IS A TYPEFACE?

A typeface is a visually distinct and consistently designed letterform of a complete alphabet, including letters, numbers, monetary symbols, and all other extended symbols. Typographers design each typeface in a way that, when the individual characters are placed side by side to form words, the letterforms aesthetically fit in any variety of combinations.

WHAT IS A FONT?

During the times of hot type, type made of lead, a font was referred to as a single character set of letters of one size, including punctuation marks, symbols, and numbers. During this time the printer's type drawer would contain multiple copies of each character, e.g., six capital *A*'s, twenty-four lowercase *a*'s, three capital *Z*'s, twenty-four lowercase *o*'s, etc. Originally, once a particular typeface was created and identified it was labeled as a "series." A series was the range of limited sizes of that typeface of the family that was manufactured in hot type, e.g., 6, 8, 10, 12, 14, 18, 24, and up to 72 points. With the advent of cold type, beginning with phototypesetting through today's desktop publishing (DTP), the word *font* has lost its original meaning somewhat. Nevertheless, in principle, a font should still refer to a particular style or character set of one size.

TYPE FAMILIES

In 1892 more than twenty hot-type foundries merged to form one large manufacturer called the American Type Foundry (ATF). With this merger, type experts were able to consolidate, organize, and establish a clear system for all of the typefaces created by the various smaller companies. It was M.F. Benton from ATF who first identified the type system called the "family." Once this system was established, many other less popular and exotic fonts found their place in the multitudes of typefaces. Benton eventually created the first type families at ATF, starting with Goudy, Cheltenham, Century, Cloister, and Stymie.

A family of type should be understood to be a group or collection of typefaces that possess a similar resemblance, very much like

Type Family	Franklin Gothic Extra Condensed
Type Family	**Franklin Gothic Condensed**
Type Family	Franklin Gothic Book
Type Family	**Franklin Gothic Demi**
Type Family	**Franklin Gothic No. 2 Roman**
Type Family	**Franklin Gothic Heavy**

Figure 3-1. Example of Franklin family of type. More Franklin family members exist but are not shown here.

a family in society today. As such, one typeface can never constitute a family of type. For example, each family should possess the same special way a serif is curved or the way an angle is proportioned or a bowl is stressed. These individual faces must, however, show some variation, such as any combination of stroke weights, like boldness or lightness; character height; width; or type posture.

The variation of words that are attached to the root name of a family name usually refers to the visual traits that make it unique, such as bold, book, light, black, semi, extra, black, condensed, and ultra-condensed, to name a few. These are the special family traits that genetically make those type family members special.

Usually one typeface is created as a model or pattern, and from this a family of typefaces is born. Some typefaces are designed from the start with the family in view, such as the typeface family called Univers created by Adrian Frutiger in 1957. The creation of other type families took place well after the original typeface was designed, like the example in Figure 3-1 called Franklin, designed by M.F. Benton in 1904.

TYPE WEIGHT, POSTURE, AND TREATMENT

TYPE WEIGHT

Type weight refers to the degree of boldness or lightness of the type form as a result of the thickness of the strokes of the lines. Examples can range from extra light to extra bold or black, with multiple variations in between. Extra thin or heavy type weights can seriously affect the degree of readability of type in larger bodies of

Eras Light	ABCDEFGXYZabcdefgxyz
Eras Medium	ABCDEFGXYZabcdefgxyz
Eras Demi	**ABCDEFGXYZabcdefgxyz**
Eras Bold	**ABCDEFGXYZabcdefgxyz**

Figure 3-2. Example of Eras typeface with its various type weights. More Eras type weights exist but are not shown here.

information. Bold, heavy, or extra heavy weight typefaces are better used in headline type where short phrases of type are used to draw attention to a larger body of text. The examples of light, medium, demi, and bold all describe the various combinations used to designate the degree of weight assigned to each character.

TYPE POSTURE

The posture of a typeface refers to how upright, slanted, or oblique it may be. This includes whether the direction is to the left or right in various degrees. The common term for type that is slanted to the left is "backslant," and the term used for a slant to the right is "italic" or "oblique."

The difference between an italic and oblique typeface is quite significant. The former is a special stylized typeface with a life of its own which was usually derived from an originally designed font. An oblique font, however, is one that has been mechanically altered to slant with no concern for the original letterform itself. The distinction between these two are especially noticeable if you compare the lowercase letters.

Times Roman Regular:	AaBbGgJjMmPpWwSs
Times Roman Italic:	*AaBbGgJjMmPpWwSs*
Times Roman Oblique:	*AaBbGgJjMmPpWwSs*
Times Roman Backslant:	AaBbGgJjMmPpWwSs

Figure 3-3. Illustration of the four possible postures that can be used in design: regular, italic, oblique, and backslant.

Small Caps	TYPE TREATMENTS CAN VARY.
All Caps	TYPE TREATMENTS CAN VARY.
Shadow	Type treatments can vary.
Outline	Type treatments can vary.

Figure 3-4. Illustration of four forms of treatment that can be given to type. Other forms exist as mentioned in this section.

TYPE TREATMENT

Treatment of type is the embellishment or manipulation of a typeface beyond its original letterform to fit a particular purpose or design. For example, it can be set as small caps, all caps, shadowed, reversed, or decorated in a variety of ways.

Type can also be distorted in proportion. Most desktop publishing systems and word processors allow type to be condensed or extended. The 10-point type in Figure 3-5 illustrates the exaggerated effect that can take place when extending or compressing type.

A major problem with using the pre-established standards provided in software, as seen in Figure 3-5, is that this form of type enhancement can distort the originally designed typeface and thereby dramatically affect the legibility of the type. In most cases, if type compression is desired, there are special typefaces that use compression and hold true to the original letterform. These typefaces are referred to as "condensed faces." Figure 3-6 shows some examples of condensed typefaces.

Example 1. Extended 200%

Be careful when using typefaces that have been extended or compressed too much.

Example 2. Extended 150%

Be careful when using typefaces that have been extended or compressed too much.

Example 3. Condensed 80%

Be careful when using typefaces that have been extended or compressed too much. Be careful when using typefaces that have been extended or compressed too much. Be careful when using typefaces that have been extended or compressed too much.

Figure 3-5. Three examples of extending or compressing type. None of these examples provide the best readability of type.

American Typewriter Condensed

Univers Ultra Condensed

Universe Extra Condensed

Gill Sans Condensed

Helvetica Condensed

Figure 3-6. Examples of condensed typefaces.

4 THE ANATOMY OF TYPE

The purpose of this chapter is to give a brief overview of the terms associated with the parts of type. As you learn the terms that describe these parts, you will develop an appreciation of the typefaces you choose in the future. Without knowing these terms, your ability to communicate with other design professionals will be limited and your confidence about font selections will be shaky.

In the diagram in Figure 4-1, you will notice the identification of particular type parts that represent the most common terms used in the type industry. You will observe that there are two basic categories of terms. The first category refers to the actual parts of the letter, e.g., serif, stem, eye, loop, ascender, and the second category refers to the form of measurement used to identify letter size, e.g., x-height, point size, cap height, etc.

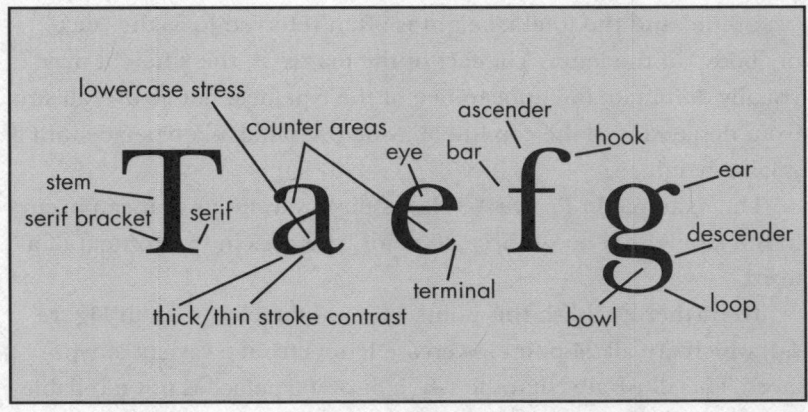

Figure 4-1. Illustration of the anatomy of type, showing the various part names of the letterform.

DETERMINING TYPE POINT SIZE

It is important to note that what designates the point size of a type-face is its measured length from the ascender or cap line to the descender line. The ascender or cap line is chosen as the topmost point based on which is the highest, as illustrated in Figure 4-2.

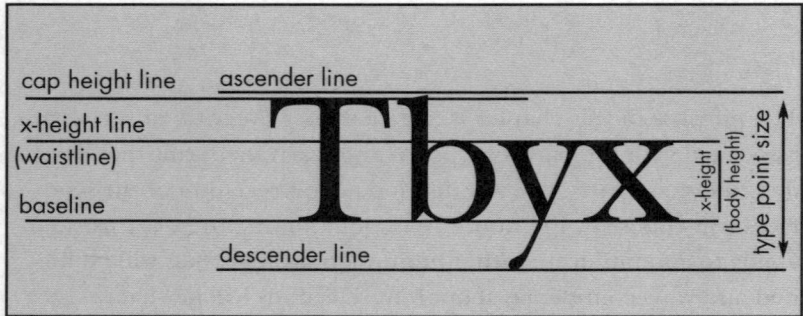

Figure 4-2. Illustration of the anatomy of type, showing the important parts and places from which to measure the letterform.

Determining what is the exact point size of a typeface can be confusing because the x-height of a typeface can vary dramatically. In other words, some typefaces appear to be larger than others because of the x-height (body height) of the letters, including height and width. The x-height line is also referred to as the type's "waistline" and the total x-height is often referred to as the "face" or "body" of the letter. The fact of the matter is, the x-height may visually dominate the appearance of the typeface, but its overall size from descender to the cap line may be the same as a typeface with a small x-height.

The example in Figure 4-3 shows three variations that can occur in the x-height of all of these 36-point typefaces in the context of a word.

To further establish this point, observe the eleven *x*'s in Figure 4-4, which are all 24-point lowercase letters from a variety of type-faces. This illustrates that the x-height of a typeface is not a reliable device by which to accurately determine a typeface's precise size. This is important because the x-height of most typefaces accounts for the majority of their size. This crucial fact reveals that the x-height of a lowercase character has a significant part in the degree of readability of words. This is especially significant because 95% of all words are in lowercase letters.

Figure 4-3. Illustration that demonstrates how the extreme variation of the x-height can change even though all three typefaces are the same point size.

Figure 4-4. Illustration that further demonstrates how the variation of the x-height can change even though these twelve different typefaces are the same point size.

5 Typographical Measuring Systems

POINTS, PICAS, THE DIDOT SYSTEM

From a historical perspective, measuring systems have provided us a way to evaluate proportion and describe quantities or values in many aspects of our everyday lives. Similarly, it is important for those who use type to have a good grasp of the terminology and application of type measuring systems.

Points. All U.S. typeface sizes are designated in points. The point system of type was developed by Pierre Simon Fournier in the U.S. in 1886. As illustrated in Figure 5-1, points identify the height and width of individual type characters. Since the proliferation of U.S. software products and the Internet, the international design and printing community has slowly become more familiar with the American system of measuring type.

Picas. Picas refer to the linear dimensions of type as they are grouped horizontally in words and sentences in a line, as well as the depth of the type area. A pica gauge is the printer's measuring tool. The corresponding systems of points to picas to inches is quite simple, as demonstrated in Figures 5-2 and 5-3.

Since the emergence of desktop publishing (DTP), there have been some slight alterations in the relationship between the inch and point systems. For example, the traditional printer's point was 0.0138 per inch, whereas PostScript points were 0.01388 per inch.

Rules. Points are also used to measure the thickness of lines, referred to as rules. The most common rules range from the hairline rules of 0.25-point (Hairline) to an 8-point rule as seen in Figure 5-4.

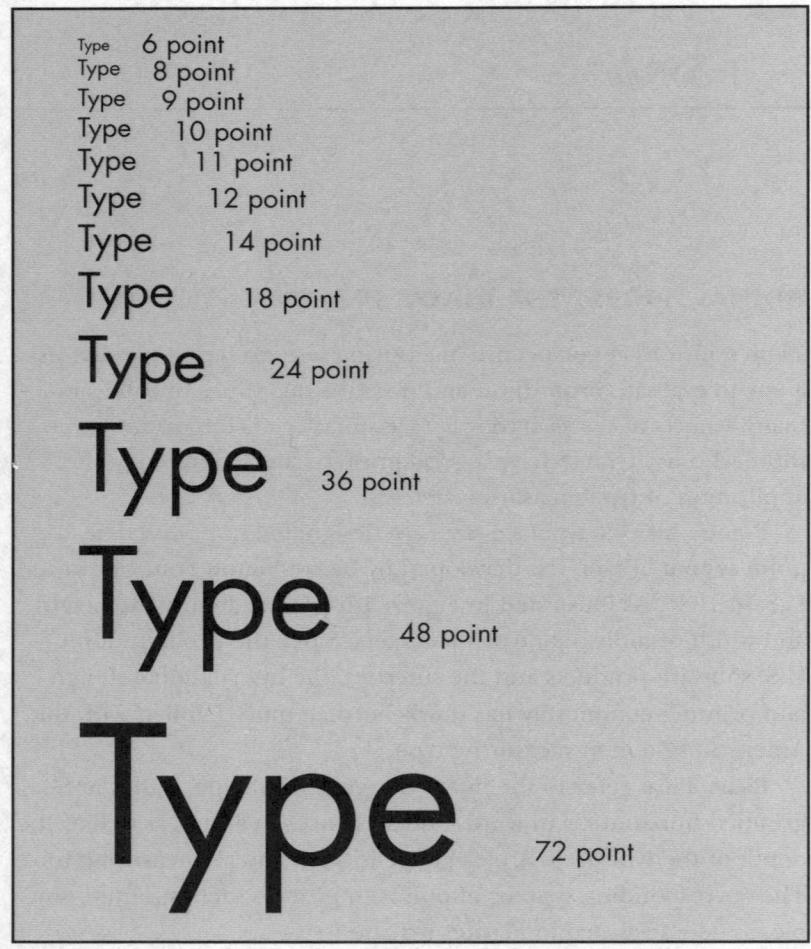

Figure 5-1. Simple illustration of 6-point to 72-point type.

The Didot System. The European type system is called the Didot point and pica system and is also referred to as the cicero system. In the Didot point system, 1 point equals 1.07 U.S. points. Most European countries, except the United Kingdom, use the U.S. point system for measuring type.

12 points	=	1 pica
6 picas	=	1 inch (1 pica = 1/6-in. approximately)
72 points	=	1 inch (approximately)
1 point	=	0.0138 inches (1/72-in. approximately)

Figure 5-2. Point–Pica–Inch ratio chart.

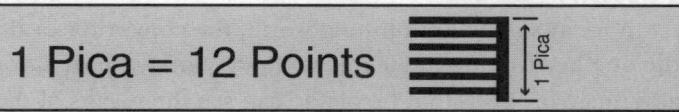

Figure 5-3. Illustration showing how many points equal 1 pica.

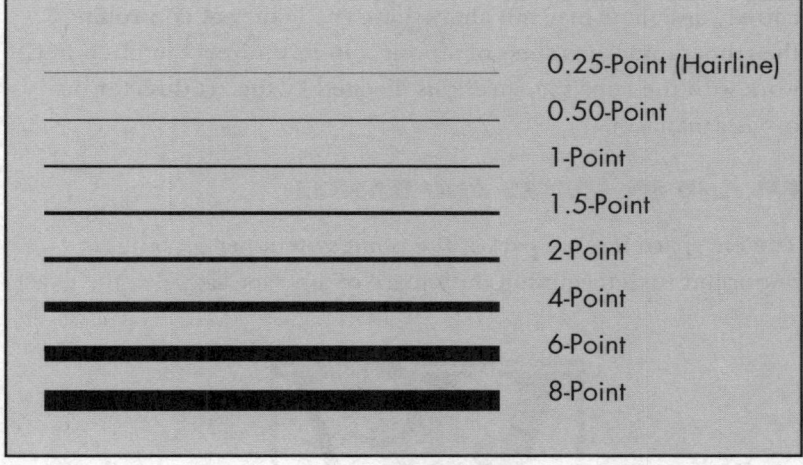

Figure 5-4. Illustration shows rule sizes measured in points.

Agate. Another form of measurement is the agate. Commonly used in the newspaper industry, the agate represents the standard for measuring the depth of all ad space, that is, the height of advertisements in newspapers and magazines. There are 14 agate lines to the inch. For example, a two-column ad 4 inches deep measures 56 agate lines and is referred to as 2 column×56 lines.

COPYFITTING

Copyfitting by itself is a slowly fading profession. Since digital publishing began to be exclusively utilized worldwide, the usefulness of copyfitting has waned considerably. Copyfitting has traditionally been used to determine the correct typeface, size, line measure, and spacing that is necessary to fit copy (text) into the available space of an anticipated page layout before type is keystroked into a typesetting device.

In today's digital publishing world, the copywriter or designer is the one keystroking the text into the designated page layout. The advantage of this is that he or she can see the results of the keystroking or importing of text immediately. From the visual results he or she can make the necessary copyfitting modifications. Of course, designers may not always have the luxury of controlling the typographic attributes of a project in its entirety but often must work with the copy specifications dictated by the art director or project manager.

EM AND EN SPACES AND DASHES

The em space is not a part of the point system per se, but it is important in determining the square of any type size, i.e., the exact

Figure 5-5. This example shows type that is 144 points vertically from the descender to the ascender, with 144 points horizontally making up one em space.

width in points. An em space is also used to measure the quantity of type within a specific page or pages.

An en space is one-half the width of the em space. Em and en spaces are usually used to indicate indention and have associated keystrokes in graphic software that can be quickly created in a body of text.

Depending on the point size of the typeface in use, the em dash is used in writing as a punctuation mark to (1) signify an interruption or transition in concept, (2) initiate an explanatory comment, or (3) connect two opposing thoughts within the same sentence.

TYPE WIDTH

Type width, also known as the "set" of a piece of type, is the narrowness in proportion to the overall letter-shape. The degree of width can range from extra-condensed to ultra-expanded with a spectrum of widths in between. The set can dramatically change the amount of text that can fit on one page. Some common terms used to describe width are *condensed, narrow, medium, ultra, extra,* and *expanded.* With the digital mechanism of the "design axis," type can retain its correct proportion and stroke width without a distortion to the original letterform.

Figure 5-6. This example shows five different typefaces that are all the same point size yet vary greatly in type width.

Example 1.

In the beginning God created the heavens and earth.
In the beginning God created the heavens and earth.

Example 2.

In the beginning God created the heavens and earth. In the
beginning God created the heavens and earth. In the beginning
God created the heavens and earth.

Example 3.

In the beginning God created the heavens and earth. In the beginning
God created the heavens and earth. In the beginning God created the
heavens and earth.

Example 4.

In the beginning God created the heavens and earth. In the beginning God created the
heavens and earth. In the beginning God created the heavens and earth. In the beginning God created the heavens and earth. In the beginning God created the heavens
and earth. In the beginning

*Figure 5-7. Notice the optical effects of various letterspace settings on the ease
of reading. Which do you prefer: Example 1, 2, 3, or 4?*

LETTERSPACE

BASIC OVERVIEW

Letterspace is the loosening and tightening of space between individual letters of a word, thereby affecting the visual balance of a
word. The visual or optical balance that is achieved through letterspacing is also referred to as "color" or "value spacing." The two
aspects of letterspacing are referred to as "negative" or "positive"
letterspace. Negative letterspace, or white-space reduction, subtracts
white space from between letters. Positive letterspacing adds space
between the letters.

Example 1. Justified Type

In the beginning God created the heavens and earth. In the beginning God created the heavens and earth. In the beginning God created the heavens and earth.

Example 2. Flush Left Type

In the beginning God created the heavens and earth. In the beginning God created the heavens and earth. In the beginning God created the heavens and earth.

Example 3. Flush Right Type

In the beginning God created the heavens and earth. In the beginning God created the heavens and earth. In the beginning God created the heavens and earth.

Example 4. Centered Type

In the beginning God created the heavens and earth. In the beginning God created the heavens and earth. In the beginning God created the heavens and earth.

Figure 5-8. Example 1, showing justified text, is a commonly used form of type arrangement. It illustrates, however, the problems that can occur when justifying larger bodies of text. Notice the larger gaps between words.

Ultimately, if the letterspacing is too loose some words may not appear to form understandable letter groups, i.e., words or phrases. This causes the spaces between the words to be difficult to discern quickly and thereby reduces the reading speed. If, however, the letterspace is too tight, the letterforms of the individual characters become difficult to distinguish from one another. This problem once again hinders the user's reading speed.

Example 1 has extremely positive letterspace and has very poor word recognition. Example 2 is slightly improved, but still has questionable word clarity. Example 3 provides the most suitable letterspace and best word recognition. Example 4 has extremely negative letterspace and, as a result, distorts the words, also giving poor word recognition.

Traditional typewriters and the early word processors could only space and separate letters equally because these older technologies were not engineered to address the finer issues of letterspace. As design software has been perfected since the mid 1980s, many of the space-related issues of typography have been automatically addressed by default. If the designer desires to further adjust the letterspace, this can be achieved through tracking or other finer devices within the software.

An additional letterspace issue depends on whether a body of text is justified, flushed to the left (ragged right) or right (ragged left), or centered. Letterspace can be adjusted easily to the correct spacing with software when it is set flush left, right, or centered. However, when type is forced to conform to a justified left and right margin, the software must calculate the best proportion of space so the type can be flush left and right simultaneously. This process takes the remaining line space and equally distributes it among the letterspace and word space within that sentence. This produces even line spacing but can also have a disproportionate and aesthetically weak typographic appearance.

LETTERSPACE OF UPPERCASE WORDS

An issue of equal concern in letterspacing is type used for display headings that contain all uppercase letters. In these cases, special letterspacing may need to be assigned to lines of type with all caps. Adding or subtracting white space from between the letters of a word directly affects the tone value of a word or group of words. These variations can drastically affect what the designer may be attempting to achieve and can have a serious impact on the degree of readability. Overall, letterspace of uppercase words should be applied differently depending on the letter groupings and context of the graphic product. The matter of legibility and readability of

Figure 5-9. Two book covers that demonstrate the use of all uppercase letters that have been spaced widely for aesthetic purposes, as seen in the author's name (in the left sample) and in the title (in the right sample).

type related to the use of uppercase letters will be discussed in more detail in Chapter 6, "The Visual Science of Type."

Although modern designers may often suspend the basic principles of letterspace, they do this with the intention of arriving at a particular aesthetic end. Regardless, this technique is only recommended for headings or small groups of words; otherwise, the eye and brain must work more than necessary to associate the group of letters to a recognizable word meaning.

For example, in the book covers in Figure 5-9, each letter was spaced to create a distinct aesthetic effect in the overall design of the cover. The typographic attributes that were considered included the balancing of the letterspace with the letter size and title and picture juxtaposition. In letterspacing of this kind, the principles of legibility were temporarily suspended to achieve a special aesthetic effect. These special exceptions must still take into consideration the principles of rhythm, harmony, and negative and positive letterspacing.

Example 1.

For example, track 1 has the most spacing, which provides the most white or positive space between characters and in appearance projects a lighter tone or color value to a page of text. Obviously, the higher the track number the denser the spacing and the darker the overall tone of the page will

Example 2.

For example, track 1 has the most spacing, which provides the most white or positive space between characters and in appearance projects a lighter tone or color value to a page of text. Obviously, the higher the track number the denser the spacing and the darker the overall tone of the page will

Example 3.

For example, track 1 has the most spacing, which provides the most white or positive space between characters and in appearance projects a lighter tone or color value to a page of text. Obviously, the higher the track number the denser the spacing and the darker the overall tone of the page will appear. For example, track 1 has the most spacing, which is

Example 4.

For example, track 1 has the most spacing, which provides the most white or positive space between characters and in appearance projects a lighter tone or color value to a page of text. Obviously, the higher the track number the denser the spacing and the darker the overall tone of the page will appear. For example, track 1 has the most spacing, which is provides the white or negative space between character and in appearance projects a lighter tone or color value to a page of text.

Figure 5-10. Example of tracking settings found in most publishing software.

TRACKING

For many students learning about type measurement, tracking can be one of the more mysterious terms because it is associated with letterspacing. However, tracking has a special function of its own that can provide a consistent pattern of letterspace assigned to larger bodies of text.

Although most publishing software has, in most cases, three basic tracks, some provide up to five or allow you to adjust the tracking to whatever degree you want. This control allows more power to be in the hands of the designer in regard to the global appearance and spacing of the text. For example, track 1 allots the most positive space between characters and, in appearance, projects a lighter tone value to a page of text. The higher the track number, the denser the spacing and the darker the tone of the page will appear. If you squint at the four examples in Figure 5-10 you will observe the text value becoming darker as the tracking increases.

KERNING

Kerning has come to be understood in general terms as mere letterspacing. However, *kerning* is the term used to designate the tightening of space between specific letters when they are used in certain combinations within a word. Kerning can be used for upper- and lowercase letters but is more often applied to uppercase letters.

The goal of kerning is to achieve a balance of optical space with the adjoining letters within a word. When letters are typed, they automatically achieve a general kind of letterspace that is calculated and appropriated by the software in use. However, in special cases the designer will have to intervene to adjust letterspace between particular characters that have not been adequately kerned.

Kerning is an important feature because it provides the designer with finer control over a balanced arrangement of letterspaces within a word. This tool can support considerable word-shape

Example 1. 2-Point Kerning

AV AW LY OA TA Ta Ty Va We Yo

Example 2. 1-Point Kerning

AV AW LY OA TA Ta Ty Va We Yo

Example 3. Auto Kerning

AV AW LY OA TA Ta Ty Va We Yo

Figure 5-11. Example of three kerning settings according to points. Which of the three examples do you feel provides the best optical kerning?

recognition when needed. This word-shape recognition increases the degree of associated word meaning from memory.

Among the hundreds of combinations Figure 5-11 shows a few examples of the letters that often need kerning to achieve the appropriate optical spacing.

WORD SPACE

In the same respect as letterspace, white space added or subtracted between words can have a dynamic effect on how quickly or easily words are read either in larger bodies of text or in display headings. Too much space between words can inhibit the reading process. Word spacing can also affect the overall tone of the text, i.e., how dark or light the text will appear and its effect on the reader's ability to grasp its meaning quickly. A general rule of thumb is that sans serif and condensed typefaces should be tighter than serif typefaces. Type experts are also guided by the "i principle" of readability with regard to word space. This rule helps to regulate the degree of calibration needed to maintain the appropriate space between words using the width of a lowercase *i* of the typeface in use.

LINE SPACE OR LEADING

Line space, commonly referred to as leading, always indicates the space between lines of the type. The origin of the term dates back to the early days of the handset typesetting composition of individual leaded characters, in which the type compositor would painstakingly build every word and sentence, letter by letter, word by word, line by line, and page by page.

Between each line of type the compositor would place a strip of metal so as not to allow the descending line to touch the ascending line of type below it, thereby allowing more white space. The line space maximized the readability of the text. This strip of metal was made of lead and created what we refer to today, even in digital typography, as leading.

Over time typographers and designers alike began to agree on a common proportion of how much leading or line space should be allotted for a particular point size of type. Today all publishing and illustration programs automatically allow for the adequate amount of leading relative to the point size of type that has been chosen. Appropriate leading can guide the eye from line to line and is a critical factor in obtaining a harmonious and functional type area that is both aesthetic and readable.

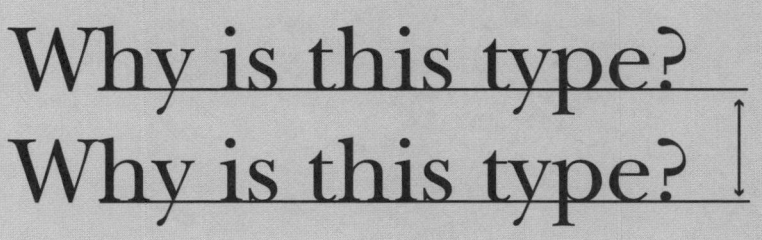

Figure 5-12. Example illustrates the way to measure leading: from baseline to baseline.

Leading is measured from baseline to baseline of the x-height. The x-height is used because the lowercase *x* provides two flat surfaces that touch the waistline and baseline within any given font. This is the most consistent way to measure leading because of variations of descender and body height among different typefaces. The illustration in Figure 5-12 shows this measurement.

6 THE VISUAL SCIENCE OF TYPE

PRINCIPLES OF VISUAL CLARITY

In an effort to maximize information recognition and retention, typographical clarity is paramount. Visual clarity is the degree by which any visual language enables readers to perceive and understand the message at hand. Designers should be concerned with typographic clarity from a "human factor" perspective; otherwise typographic decisions based on pure subjectivity may skew the perception of the reader.

A distinction should be drawn between "legibility" and "readability," because these words are often used synonymously. In principle, "legibility" is related to the optical perception of the form of individual characters or letterforms, whereas "readability" is the optical perception of groups of letters that have been formed into words and/or sentences. These are crucial distinctions because the printed page is often more legible than readable due to a designer's or organization's lack of concern for a reader's ease and speed of reading.

Although quantitative research has provided us with a firm foundation from which to make typographic decisions, measuring the legibility of type can still have some degree of fluctuation because of four perceptual dimensions. These variations consist of (1) the reader's comprehension level of the text (related to age and reading level), (2) the cultural makeup of the readers, (3) the perceptual context in which the reader encounters the text, and (4) the informational context or familiarity that the reader has with the text.

Given that all of these factors generally can be controlled, a scientific approach to analyzing type can provide us a more reliable measuring device by which to gauge word recognition and speed and ease of reading. Hence, it is important to understand the difference between two factors that have a significant impact on maintaining the visual clarity of type, i.e., legibility and readability. Both factors play a direct role in balancing aesthetic decisions, which often have a tendency to dominate typographical judgment.

LEGIBILITY

Legibility is concerned with the perception of individual letters and words and is defined by the measurement of (1) the ease of perception among typefaces and (2) the distinction of one letterform from another within a group or cluster of words, e.g., headlines, item lists, headings of various kinds, even a street sign or billboard. To arrive at optimum legibility one should ask, "Have my typographic decisions provided the reader a way to immediately find, identify, recognize, and retain the word or word groupings with considerable success and without confusion?"

An important factor that affects legibility is the shape of a word. When words are set in all caps they are less legible, whether the typeface is serif or sans serif. Setting text in all caps often creates a breakdown in visual clarity because word recognition is based on word-shape and not letter size.

When words are set in all uppercase characters, the mind reads it first as a rectangular shape rather than a uniquely formed word-shape created by the variation in lowercase letters. This word-shape variation gives each word its own optical identity. In lowercase words, the ascenders and descenders extend beyond the x-height of the word, becoming more distinct in form. All uppercase words line up along their baseline and cap line, forming a perfect box, which forces the reader to decode each individual character before understanding the word. This cognitive process uses more brain process-

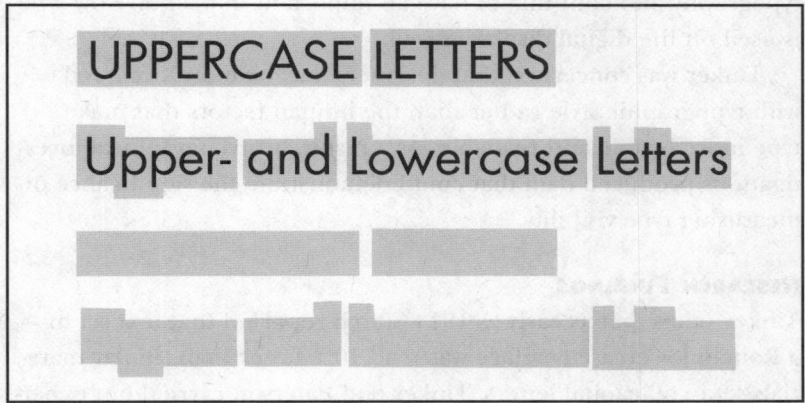

Figure 6-1. Examples illustrating the comparison of the word-shape between all uppercase and upper-/lowercase words.

ing power and time in addition to being a strain on the eyes. This is illustrated by the example in Figure 6-1.

LEGIBILITY RESEARCH

Since early in the twentieth century, psychologists like M.A. Tinker have done extensive research in the area of legibility and readability of print. Tinker's classic text, titled *Legibility of Print,* is one of the first foundational works that provided designers and typographers with much of the early scientific data to substantiate the important issues that surround the typographic attributes that can either inhibit or promote the legibility and readability of type.

Tinker's studies investigated the human factors that affect word recognition, information retention, reading speed, and recognition of letterforms. Overall, these studies revealed that, for larger bodies of text, serif letterforms provide an ease of reading unequaled by sans serif typefaces. On the other hand, sans serif typefaces provide an ability to make a direct and immediate connection to the reader's word-recognition processes for understanding word meaning. In other words, the evenly stroked letterforms of most sans serifs evoke an immediate understanding from the reader. Tinker's findings paved the way for the establishment of standards for good typography and continue to have an important impact on how type is used on the digital display as well.

Tinker was concerned that designers may be more occupied with typographic style rather than the human factors that make type more legible and readable. As a result, his typographical investigations produced data that could demonstrate the significance of measuring type visibility.

RESEARCH FINDINGS

Tinker states that as early as 1914 Starch reported that text set in a Roman lowercase typeface was read 10% faster than similar materials set in all capital letters. Tinker and Paterson carried out experiments with 320 readers comparing lowercase to uppercase text and showed the exact same trend. Figure 6-3 shows the table from Tinker's *Legibility of Print* which demonstrates this fact.

READABILITY

Readability is related to the arrangement and reading of continuous textual materials and is measured by the degree of speed and ease by which a body of text can be read and understood. Type is either high or low on the readability scale. To arrive at optimum readability, one should ask, "Have my typographic decisions provided the reader a way to discriminate the word forms perceived accurately, rapidly, easily, and with clear understanding?"

Letterspace, word space, type size, color, weight, stroke, thickness, posture, shape, texture, serif/sans serif, contour, leading, and length of text line all add to how readable a body of text will be. In other words, these various attributes used in any number of combinations can significantly hinder the ease by which text is read. As a result, a careful selection of typographic attributes can promote or hinder word-shape recognition, which affects the ability to gather meaning from the text.

Ultimately, a properly designed page of text should become transparent to the eye, making the range of typographic features virtually unnoticeable during the reading process. If the opposite

SPEED OF READING		
Type Case	Average No. Paragraphs Read	Difference in Percent
Lowercase	18.83	–11.8
Uppercase	16.61	–11.8
READER OPINIONS OF RELATIVE LEGIBILITY		
Type Case	Average Rank	Percentage Choice
Lowercase	1.1	90
Uppercase	1.9	100

Table 4.6. Legibility of all capitals versus lowercase.

Figure 6-3. Table from Tinker's text, Legibility of Print, outlines the speed of reading and reader opinion.

Example 1. Upper-Lowercase Characters

This is a sample of how easy or difficult it can be when attempting to read type that is set in all caps. You make the choice. Which is easier to read? Type that is in all uppercase is the least legible.

Example 2. All Uppercase Characters

THIS IS A SAMPLE OF HOW EASY OR DIFFICULT IT CAN BE WHEN ATTEMPTING TO READ TYPE THAT IS SET IN ALL CAPS. YOU MAKE THE CHOICE. WHICH IS EASIER TO READ? TYPE THAT IS IN ALL UPPERCASE IS THE LEAST LEGIBLE.

Figure 6-4. Two examples show the degree of readability between uppercase and lowercase letters and all uppercase letters.

occurs, then the letters or words have become overstated and more distinctive than necessary. These distinctions can result in a low degree of readability. This is not to say that any given page layout cannot have a primary focal point, but overall the body of text employed must maintain optimum readable quality to make the reading effortless.

READABLE TYPE POINT SIZE

As discussed earlier, there are point sizes that have proven to be the most readable. Most designers agree that 9- to 12-point type should be used for reading material, with 10- to 11-point being optimal. This can vary depending on the typeface chosen or whether it is serif or sans serif. A proper balance between the visual science of type and aesthetics should govern the choice of typeface style, size, and attribute.

READABLE TYPEFACES

Research has shown that many of the older typefaces with moderate letterform features make the most readable text. Some excellent examples of this are Times Roman, Palatino, Minion, and Garamond, many of which were originally designed in the fifteenth and sixteenth centuries. Many of these typefaces have become the proven and true letterforms that effortlessly glide the reader forward word by word because of their carefully designed letterforms and the use of serifs. Serifs help to guide the eye comfortably from letter-shape to letter-shape.

Serifs help guide the eye effortlessly.

Figure 6-5. Lighter gray areas show how serifs guide the eye along from letter-shape to letter-shape and from word-shape to word-shape.

The earliest experiments done by Tinker on readability consisted of nine hundred readers who compared serif, sans serif, and Old English typefaces. Using Scotch Roman (similar to Times

Variation in Speed of Reading Ten Typefaces

Typeface	% Differences
Garamond	+ 0.4
Scotch Roman (Standard)	− 0.0
Antique	− 0.2
Bodoni	− 1.0
Old Style	− 1.1
Caslon Old Style	− 1.3
Kabel Light	− 2.2
Cheltenham	− 2.4
American Typewriter	− 4.7
Cloister Black (Old English)	−13.6

Figure 6-6. Speed reading test data from readability research by M.A. Tinker. Garamond provides the greatest readability, and Cloister Black provides the lowest readability.

Ten Typefaces Ranked According to Reader Preference

Typeface	Average Rank	Rank Order
Cheltenham	2.2	1
Antique	2.4	2
Bodoni	4.2	3
Old Style	4.6	4
Garamond	5.4	5
American Typewriter	5.5	6
Scotch Roman (Standard)	6.2	7
Caslon Old Style	6.4	8
Kabel Light	8.2	9
Cloister Black (Old English)	9.8	10

Figure 6-7. Ranking according to the reader's personal preference of typefaces used in readability test.

Roman) as the standard, nine other typefaces were compared. The results unequivocally revealed that serif typefaces increased reading speed. The Roman to Caslon typefaces, which are Old Style serif typefaces, had similar results, with some of the best reading speeds being allowed by Garamond. Beginning with the Kabel, a sans serif typeface, there was a noticeable decrease in reading speed. The American Typewriter typeface showed a noticeable double degradation in reading speed. Cloister Black, an Old English typeface, showed the rate of reading speed was 13% worse. The table in Figure 6-6 shows the results of this experiment.

The fascinating thing is that Tinker also asked the same nine hundred readers for their preference with regard to the same ten typefaces. In other words, he inquired as to what typeface they personally felt was more pleasing to read. Their preferences did not match the typefaces that yielded the best results in the speed-of-reading experiment. This additional "personal taste" test revealed that subjective preference is not a safe guide for determining visual clarity or the degree of readability.

The reader's top choice among the ten typefaces was Cheltenham, which conversely ranked eighth in readability. Garamond, which was ranked first for reading speed, was chosen as a mere medium choice, almost ranking the same as American Typewriter, which reduced the reading speed by four times. The chart in Figure 6-7 reveals this data.

The lesson designers should learn from this documented experiment is that personal preference in typography does not always provide optimal readability of text. This fact must guide the designer in type choices that are a balance between aesthetic taste and scientific judgment.

TYPE SIZE AND LEADING PROPORTIONS

A factor that is related to maximizing smooth transitional eye movement during reading is the relative proportion between type size, leading, and line length. If the leading is not adequate, consecutive

Example 1.
Appropriate leading can guide the eye from line to line and is a critical factor in obtaining a harmonious and functional type area that is
both aesthetically and optically pleasing.

Example 2.
Appropriate leading can guide the eye from line to line and is a critical factor in obtaining a harmonious and functional type area that is
both aesthetically and optically pleasing.

Example 3.
Appropriate leading can guide the eye from line to line and is a critical factor in obtaining a harmonious and functional type area that is
both aesthetically and optically pleasing.

Example 4.
Appropriate leading can guide the eye from line to line and is a critical factor in obtaining a harmonious and functional type area that is
both aesthetically and optically pleasing.

Figure 6-8. Example of 10-point type set at 10.5-, 12-, 13.5-, and 16-point
leading. Which example do you feel is the most readable?

eye tracking from line to line will be more difficult. If the type size
is increased, both the leading and line length can also increase. In
this case, to maintain readability, standard leading and line length
should increase proportionately.

Another leading rule is related to the amount of lines of type on
a page. The more leading there is the fewer lines of type should be
allowed per page. There is a balance that should transpire between
the demand to conserve space and the readability of the text. A
common rule is the greater the line length the greater the required
line space. In principle the line space should be at least 1/30th of
the line length. If the lines are spaced too closely together, the eye
has a more difficult time moving from line to line.

Example 1. The Worst Line Length for This Size Type
The size of your type should determine the proper
leading to achieve the highest level of readability.
The size of

Example 2. Still Not Enough Line Length for This Size Type
The size of your type should determine the proper leading to
achieve the highest level of readability. The size of your type

Example 3. This Approaches the Best Line Length for This Size Type
The size of your type should determine the proper leading to achieve the highest level of readability. The size of your type should determine the
proper

*Figure 6-9. Example of 14-point type set at various line
lengths.*

7 TYPOGRAPHY AND GRID SYSTEMS

GRID SYSTEM BASICS

THE DESIGNER AND THE GRID SYSTEM

A great advantage of the grid system is the discipline it can impose on the designer who is first attempting to learn the principles of sound typographic composition. When the young designer is just beginning to form the proper understanding of two-dimensional space, the grid will train him/her how to divide, subdivide, and analyze the various spaces to arrive at a cohesive, well-balanced, and harmonious design solution.

Designers must learn to work with a variety of shapes which can work within the confines of a variety of page formats. The designer should know the exact measurements of the physical requirements, the various elements that will be used in the arrangement, and the degree of emphasis that the various elements will need. A grid system should then be considered and developed relative to these factors. The grid, however, should not become a dominant factor that controls or forces the typography into a rigid, unyielding structure but should act as a hidden skeleton that serves the designer, not that the designer must serve. If we use the grid merely as an instrument of good design, it should be used with flexibility and modified to fit the creative needs of the designer.

The grid should match the designer's style of working as well as the predetermined requirements established for the graphic or information-based product. The designer should always keep in mind that the grid should be constructed to be a simple visual outline or system for a large variety of typographic and pictorial elements while providing relative continuity. Nevertheless, the quality of the completed design must be evaluated by its resulting form and function and not by the complexity of the grid.

THE PURPOSE OF GRID SYSTEMS

The study of the proportions of the human body has played a significant role in how we look at two-dimensional space and ultimately the use of grid systems. As long as mathematics has been part of our system of measurement, grid systems have provided a basic framework for architecture, the arts, and typographic form. Beginning with the first typefaces designed for the printing press, typographers used grids to design letter-shapes and complete the layout of the printed page. Johann Gutenberg's forty-two-line Bible was formed with a precise grid system (Figure 7-2).

What makes the use of grids so important is their ability to create a system of proportion and the means to solve complex design problems. It has been scientifically proven that information is more quickly and easily accessed using a system that conforms to a consistent and cohesive format. To create page layouts with harmony, mechanical form, and practical application, aesthetics cannot be the only consideration. Both systematic principles of proportion and aesthetic intuition should jointly bear the undergirding of a sound typographic layout. As a result, the design should create a grid based on aesthetic judgment and scientific analysis of the shapes, proportions, and dimensions of the space to be organized.

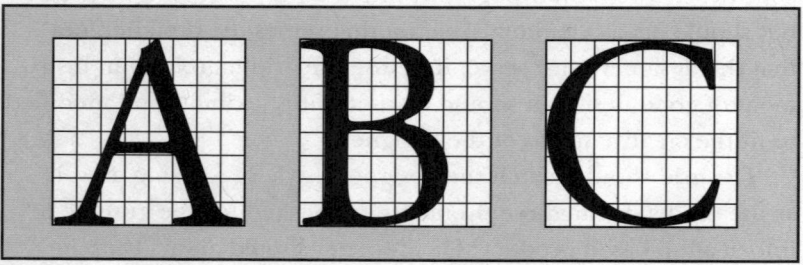

Figure 7-1. Illustration of how an underlying grid was used to design and guide the creation of letterforms.

This fact has been validated by centuries of mathematicians, artists, designers, and architects from Greek antiquity to the Renaissance to the Modern Age.

Grid systems are used by typographers, graphic designers, photographers, industrial designers, and graphic technologists for solving a variety of visual problems in two- and three-dimensional

Figure 7-2. An evident grid system can been seen in Gutenberg's forty-two-line Bible designed in the fifteenth century in Germany.

space. By constructing space with a grid system, the designer is able to arrange the text, photographs, diagrams, and other visual elements according to the functionality of the product. The nine points which follow summarize the purpose of grid systems.

Framework: Grid systems divide a two- or three-dimensional space into a number of smaller areas or fields that serve as an underlying structure to establish guides for the design and placement of typographic and graphic elements.

Order/Visual Clarity: Grid systems establish visual clarity and a predictable visual ordering system that can navigate the user through two- and three-dimensional fields of space.

Organization/Planning: Grid systems convey a well-organized and thought-out structure for text and illustrations and also provide a systematic presentation of facts or sequence of events throughout a unified visual work.

Unity/Cohesion: Grid systems promote a sense of unity and cohesion between type and other graphics within a page or the screen display layout.

Control/Consistency: Grid systems determine and control the dimensions of space, giving a sense of spatial consistency throughout.

Problem-solving: Grid systems provide the designer a systematic means through which to more quickly solve simple and complex visual problems.

Rhythm/Harmony: Grid systems can provide repeated visual rhythm and harmony throughout an entire work.

Uniformity/Intelligibility: Grid systems give a sense of uniformity, which in fact suggests an intelligibility of design.

Credibility/Confidence: A well-planned grid system gives credibility to the information in use and can strongly suggest confidence in the overall quality of the graphic product at hand.

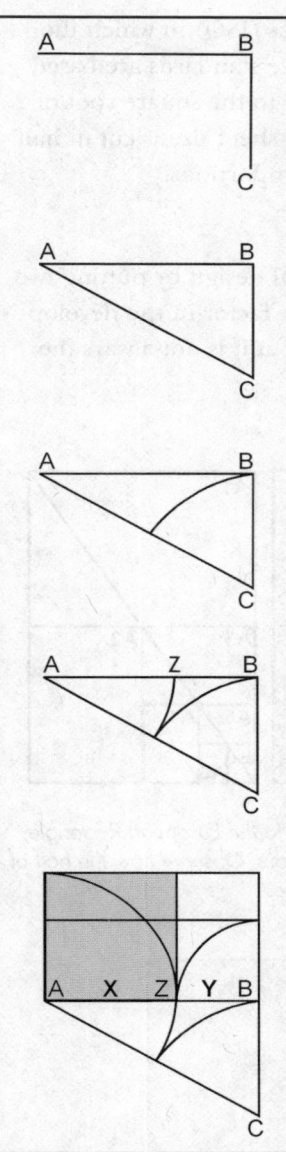

Figure 7-3. Illustration of the steps employed to create the Golden Rectangle.

GRID SYSTEM PAGE FORMATS

The square is the simplest of all formats, and it is a rectangle that provides us the natural division of the Golden Rectangle, European Rectangle, and the Japanese Double Square.

GOLDEN RECTANGLE

The Golden Rectangle is formed by drawing a triangle using one-half the width of the horizontal line (AB) to create the vertical line (BC). Join the two ends to form an enclosed triangle (AC). Draw an arc on an axis where the horizontal and vertical lines meet (B), using the bottom of the vertical line (C) as your center point. Using A as a center point, draw an arc on the AZ axis. Draw another arc upward from the new location marked Z on the perpendicular line on the triangle to form the vertical line of a box. Where the curve bisects A and B, it will divide the baseline into the extreme X and the mean Y. When we use X as the shorter side of a rectangle and AB as the long side, a Golden Rectangle is formed.

EUROPEAN RECTANGLE

The European Rectangle is drawn by creating an extension of the square along the arc of its diagonal. This rectangle also provides the basis of the European paper size standard A series.

Europe uses the international paper sizes (ISO) in which the metric system is the standard. ISO paper size standards are based on a rectangle whose sides have a ratio of 1 to the square root of 2 (1:1.414) regardless of how many times the sheet size is cut in half. So each half will always keep its constant proportions.

JAPANESE SQUARE

The Japanese Square forms an asymmetrical design by putting two squares together. The square is also a major factor in the development of the grid for designers and artists, but it is not always the shape most commonly used.

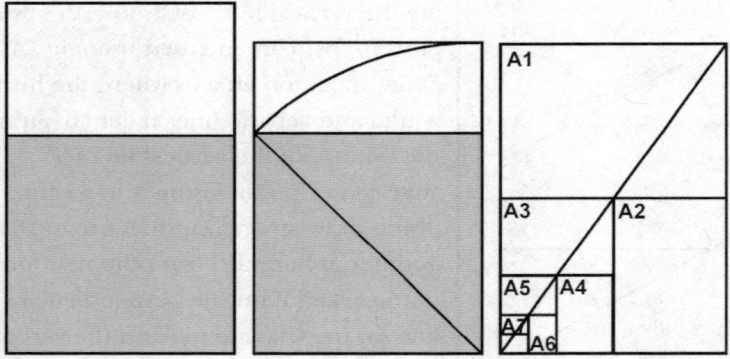

Figure 7-4. A comparison of the Golden Rectangle to the European Rectangle, as well as the various sizes of the European Rectangle. Observe how the half of each whole repeatedly creates the same size in ratio.

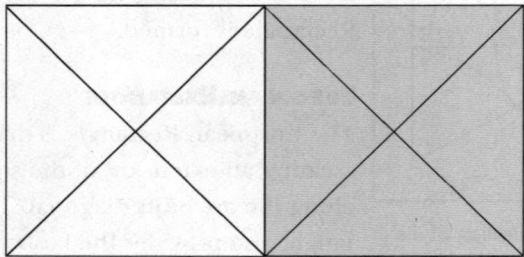

Figure 7-5. Illustration of the Japanese Square doubled.

AMERICAN AND EUROPEAN SHEET SIZES COMPARED

The format on which the designer creates the layout for type can vary. There are, however, standard proportions that are used in America and Europe that are important to know. In the U.S. and the United Kingdom, paper sizes are measured in inches, whereas the rest of Europe uses another system, as mentioned previously. The most common size in Europe is the A4 size, which is approximately 8.25×11.75-in. or 210×297-mm. Within both standard formats, the depth and width of the columns are mathematically measured using a typographic system of points, picas, or cicero (European system). The two systems illustrated in Figure 7-6 show the common sizes that are used in both America and Europe.

PRINCIPLES OF GRID SYSTEM CONSTRUCTION

The division of the space within the grid system should begin with the margins, i.e., on the left, right, top, and bottom side edges of the format. The format should then be divided into a broader number of columns, then rows as needed. There can be any number of columns, beginning with two and going up to eight if necessary,

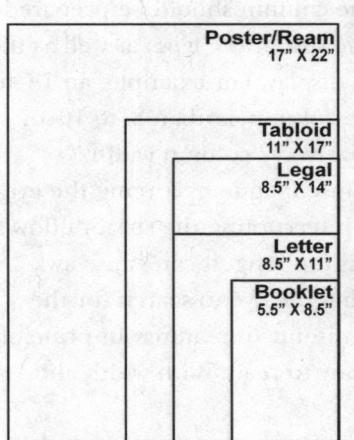
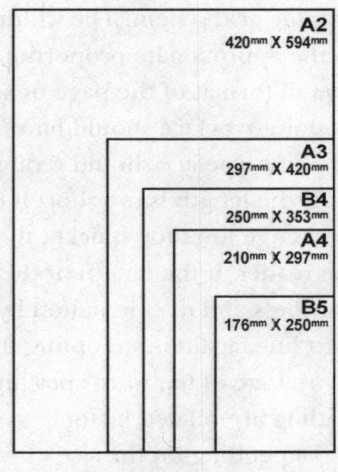

Figure 7-6. Illustration that compares the American and European paper sizes and their similar proportions.

depending on the overall width of the format. The columns are used primarily for text, so the rules of legibility play a significant part in determining the number of words that will be in one column width. The range of columns and subdivisions of these columns is up to the designer, who will determine how complex the grid should be. Another factor is whether the format will be a single page or will have facing or multiple pages. This adds another factor that can influence the style and complexity of the grid system.

Depending on whether you are designing a book, magazine, brochure, or screen display, the grid system will vary according to the basic elements incorporated. The placement of traditional design elements should be considered, e.g., page numbering; headers; footers; margin width; hierarchy of information; and, in the case of interface design, website navigation.

ELEMENTS OF THE GRID SYSTEM

COLUMN WIDTH

Designing a column width for type that is both pleasing to the eye and optically correct is a challenge when planning a typographic grid system. The width of the column should be prepared to the approximate proportion of the size of the type, as well as the overall format of the page or screen display. For example, an 18- to 24-point typeface should have a wide column, and an 8- to 10- or 11-point typeface should require a narrower column width.

If the length is too short it can cause fatigue by forcing the eye to change lines too quickly, thereby interrupting the smooth flow to the reader. If the length of the line is too long, it can cause awkwardness and disorientation by forcing the eye to search for the next line, again interrupting the continuity of reading. In principle, an average of ten words per line is easy to read. Both width and leading are related factors.

Depending on the size of type selected for reading, researchers have calculated that there should be approximately eight to twelve

Example 1. Not Good

The concept of chunking should be applied to line lengths that conform to the typeface size that are in use in the portions to be chunked.

Example 2. Better

That is, relative proportions should match between the line length and type size to promote textual chunking that allows eye movement to move down to the next line without undue disorientation.

Example 3. Best

That is, relative proportions should match between the line length and type size to promote textual chunking that allows eye movement to move down to the next line without undue disorientation. That is, relative proportions should match between...

Figure 7-7. Three examples of line length.

words per line. Lines that are longer than this make it more difficult for the reader to retrack eye movement to the following line location, thereby slowing down the reading. If a larger type point size is used, then longer lines can be used. Less than this allows too much eye movement from line to line.

MARGIN PROPORTIONS

Every typographic area must be surrounded with a white or non-text zone. This neutral zone is referred to as the margin. The purpose of building adequate margins into a grid system is to enhance the typographic legibility of the text. Margins optically allow the text to have more breathing space, thereby providing the reader ease of reading within a well-proportioned format that is engulfed by an open space.

Margins should not be made too narrow. A common mistake of young designers is to make narrow margins, thereby pushing the text areas very close to the edge of the page. This disrupts the equilibrium of text and non-text zones and gives the feeling that the page is too full. The seasoned designer will always include in the

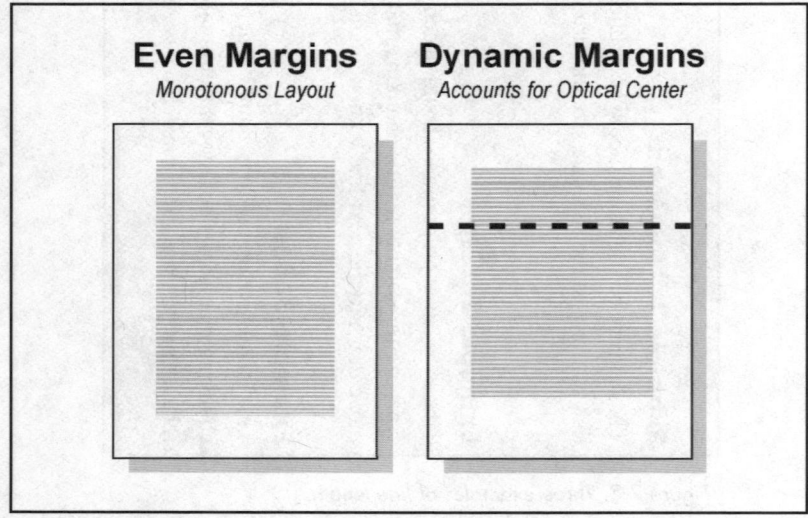

Figure 7-9. Illustration of the single page format with margins.

layout grid the maximum amount of space to maintain a dynamic tension within the proportions of text and white space. This area can vary depending on the size of the format, the size of the text area, the quantity of the text, and/or any degree of other variables caused by other images, tone, or color. There are, however, some rule-of-thumb principles that can be used as a guide. These principles are as follows.

General. There should be consistency in the starting point or the location of where type begins from page to page. There must be enough white space above the text so that it is proportional to the page size. If a page has relatively little text but the type is large, the margins should be wide.

Single-page Margins. Depending on where the margin is located (top, bottom, left, right), it can function differently and have a different designation. In a single-page format, the left and right margins are the same, the top margin should have a little more than the sides, and the bottom is given more space than the top. The variation in margin proportions is done because the optical center of the page is slightly higher than the mathematical center; therefore, there should be an adjustment. This adjustment allows for and conveys a more pleasing proportion of text-to-margin space.

Thumb-space Margins. When designing a two-page spread, the proportionate design of margins becomes more complex. In the facing-page format, i.e., pages that are facing one another, the outer margins are the same width on the left side of the left page and on the right side of the right page. These margins are called the thumb-space margins. The margins where the two pages come together are the inner margins and should also be the same in width.

The exact place where the two pages come together is called the gutter. The gutter is the place where the pages are bound together or are folded, depending on the construction of the graphic product. There is often an extra allotment of margin space in the gutter because the bound or folded product may not be able to lie flat, thereby diminishing the actual optical margin space.

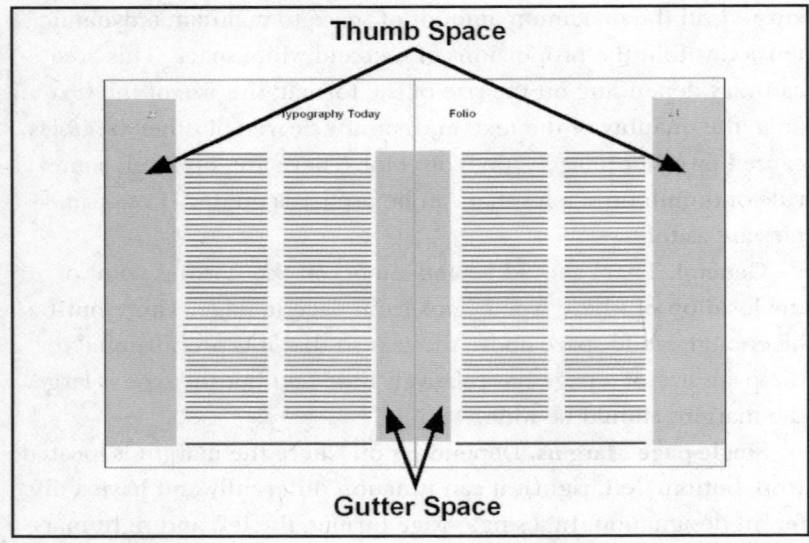

Figure 7-9. Illustration of facing pages with thumb-space and gutter-space margin locations.

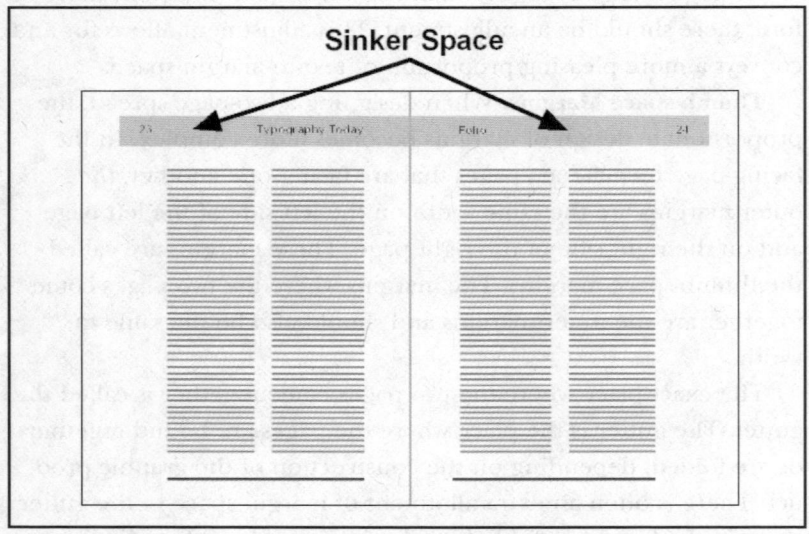

Figure 7-10. Illustration of the page format with necessary foot-space margins.

Sink or Foot-space Margins. The margin space at the top of a page is called the sink. The sink area contains the header information, often being the title of the book, chapter title, part title, and/or page number. The footer space is the margin at the bottom of the page and can also be the location of the same information as the header, but information is never repeated. Some publications may even have a combination of both, e.g., the title information in the sink area, being the header, with the page numbers located in the footer space. This, of course, is a judgment call on the part of the designer.

LEADING IN RELATION TO COLUMN DEPTH

Properly calculated leading between the lines of type is a critical factor for maintaining the ease and speed of reading when considered in relation to column width. If the lines are too closely set, the eye will take in the surrounding lines and thereby frustrate the continuity of the reading. In relation to grid systems, the typographic consideration of leading is an additional factor in the proportional design of a format.

PAGE NUMBERING

Establishing a location on the grid for placement of page numbers, also referred as a "folio," is an important typographic decision both functionally and aesthetically. As mentioned earlier, a folio can be placed in the footer or header space of the grid. When choosing the location of the folio, experts have observed that optical dynamics are more readily achieved when the folio is placed in the far left or far right page location. Centering the folio exactly in the middle of each page may appear to be a safe folio location, but it will give a static and monotonous impression. By choosing these far-edge locations on the page, the eye more quickly turns to the extremities of the format space because of the optical weight in either direction, given the layout has the adequate left and right margin space.

Whether the folio is placed above, below, to the left, or to the right of the text area, the amount of space that separates it from

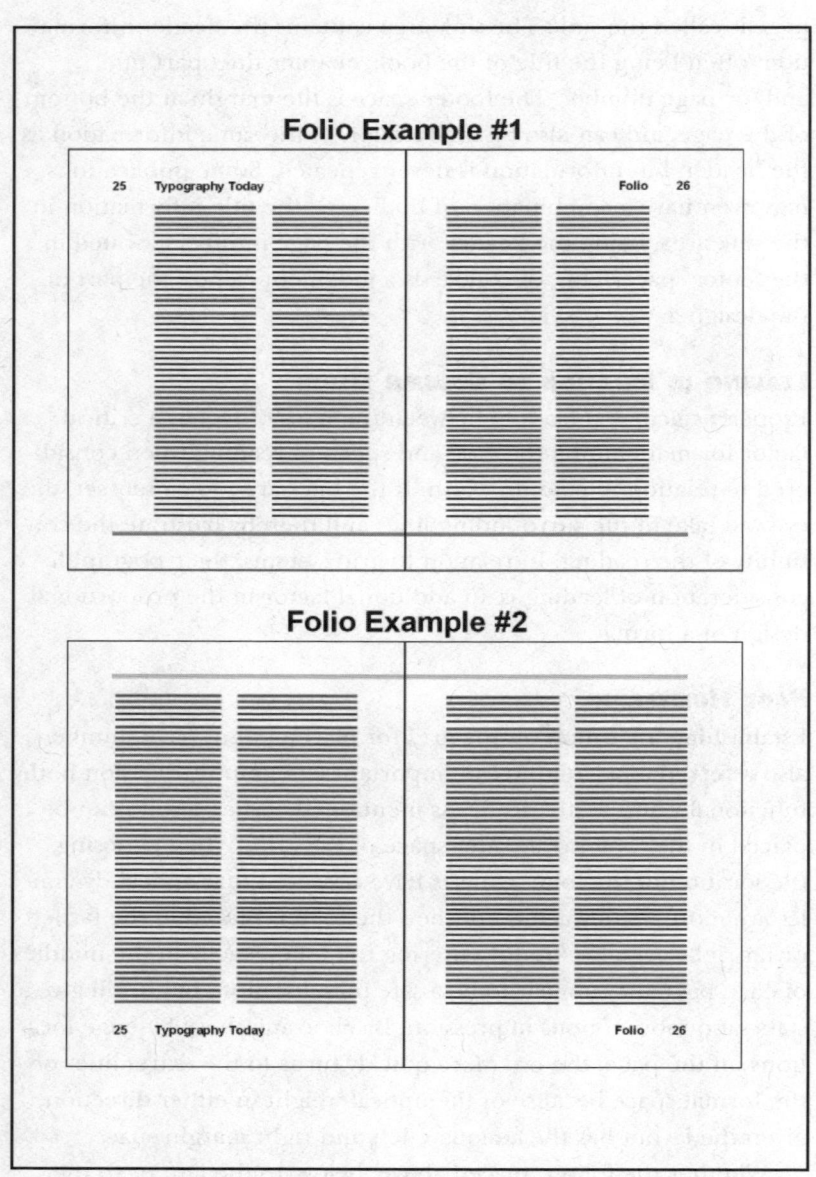

Figure 7-11. Two examples the best folio locations.

the text should be approximately the same as the space between columns. In other words, the folio should not be placed too far from the body of type or it could go unnoticed.

BODY TYPE

The main typographic section of the page format is the body text. The proportion of the body text to the overall size of the page should be controlled largely by the necessary margin space that should be allowed for a proper balance between type and white space.

The actual size and placement of the body text should be determined mostly by the amount of text and its proportionate size within the grid. If the typographic layout has a small amount of text but a large format, the design can be quite liberal with the margin space, but if the opposite is true, more careful consideration must be made so as not to give the reader a cramped feeling, which can directly contribute to lowering the degree of readability.

8 TYPOGRAPHIC DEVICES FOR OPTIMIZING VISUAL COMMUNICATION

TEXTUAL CHUNKING

Chunking is a specific technique that improves visual clarity by shortening text into groups of sentences that have been clustered together. Specifically, chunked line lengths of concise and particularly related ideas can contribute to a more rapid ingestion and comprehension of textual information.

Textual researchers have found, in addition to considering typographic styles, attributes, and spacing for optimum readability, chunking discrete portions of text can increase the factors that contribute to reading speed and information retention. The concept of chunking has been identified by M.A. Tinker as an influence on improving reading comprehension, making it more functional through a deliberate emphasis on form. Tinker's research revealed that readers were able to optically grasp chunks of text when they where in shorter, more concise portions.

This especially applies to learning materials in textbooks, presentations, or in Web navigation, particularly in conjunction with hypertext. Based on these studies, an emphasis should not only be placed on reading speed but also on reading that is both easy and interesting. If the portion of text is too large it should be reviewed again to determine a way to divide it into smaller parts.

In essence, chunking helps the user deal with one idea at a time by presenting one well-defined packet of information at a time, whether on a printed page or on a Web page.

TEXTUAL CUEING

In any typographical composition, whether for print or display, textual cueing can provide an additional tool by which to improve reading comprehension and speed. Textual cueing is a visual apparatus that signals change to the reader. In the broader sense, textual cueing does not include only the obvious graphic changes that occur in chapters or part openings of books, pamphlet, booklets, etc., but rather involves the more subtle changes that occur within the complexity of larger bodies of textual information. These larger volumes of information often need further visual clarification to guide and alert the reader to change or new information. These areas can be sections, subsections, and/or highlighted notes.

Textual cueing is first created by maintaining consistency in the layout and visual attributes of the page format, especially related to

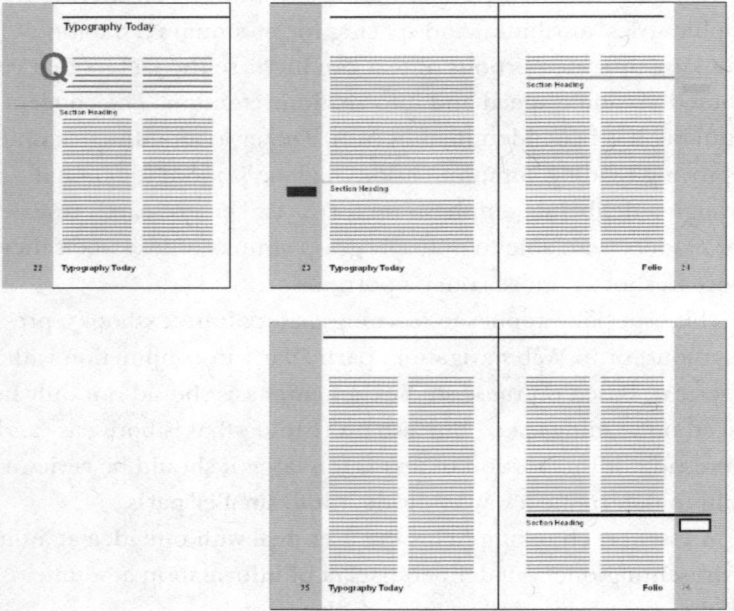

Figure 8-1. Illustration of textual cueing by page maintaining visual consistency and then making changes to a variety of graphic elements.

the application of typographic elements and attributes. As these factors are intentionally altered, the user is cued as to a change of content or direction in the textual information.

More complex cueing can include more intricate systems of textual color-coding or any other organized selection of typographic attributes that alert the reader to change within the body of text. Special use of textual cueing can take on an important role in instructional or information-based graphics that must effectively display an abundance of complex information.

VISUAL HIERARCHY

Typography plays an important part in the visual hierarchy of information management. The responsibility of visual communication is to produce a cohesive and consistent hierarchy of information to smoothly guide the reader's eye page by page. In such a layout, content is organized logically where the reader can predictably proceed with minimal disorientation. As discussed earlier, a well thought-out grid can assist in this kind of ordering system.

HIERARCHICAL VISUAL COGNITION

To achieve the optimum effect in the hierarchy of information, specific devices should be employed. It is, however, important to understand first the basic cognitive processes that the eye and brain engage in as they scan a page of textual and graphic information. We will refer to this process as *hierarchical visual cognition*.

During the process of stepping through such a hierarchy of visual information, the reader proceeds through three progressive stages to arrive at a coherent recognition of the layout containing type and graphics.

First, the reader's eye quickly moves across the page, scanning and registering the basic images to the brain. This first glance is seen as an arrangement of larger shapes that project what may optically appear to be foreground and background elements in various degrees of contrast. Second, the eye scans the page again, registering more information and picking up more refined visual detail

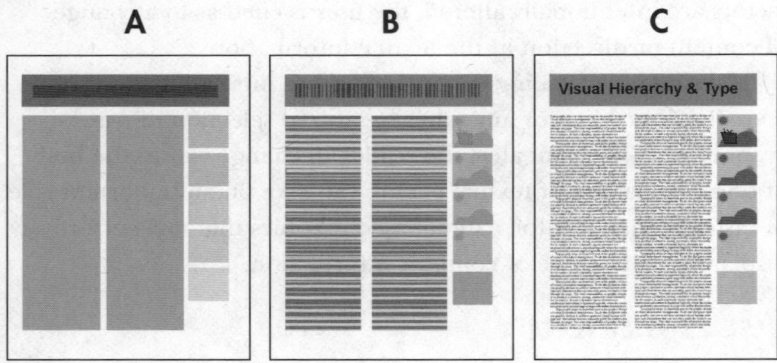

Figure 8-2. Illustration shows: A. Eye movement first scans page, registering a basic image to the brain. B. Eye scans page with more refined result, giving text-improved definition. C. Eye finally scans page with true definition of text and images.

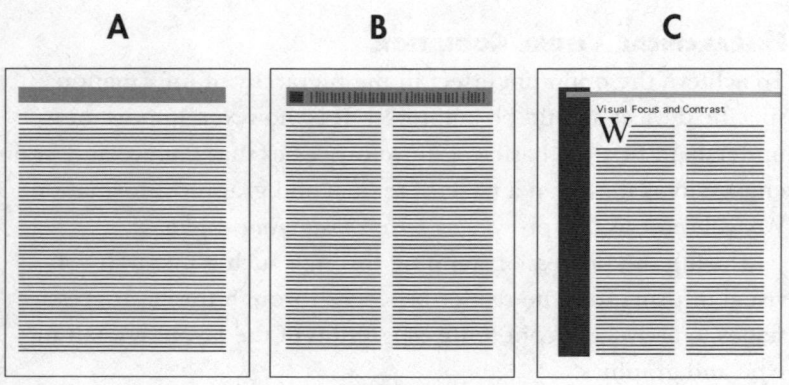

Figure 8-3. Illustration shows: A. Visually flat with no focus or contrast. B. Increased contrast, less monotonous, but still lacks dynamics. C. Visual focus, contrast, and elements of balance and sophistication come into play.

that gives both text and graphic information more definition and form. In the third stage, the optical and cognitive processes reach a point where letterforms, words, and chunks of information (phrases) can be parsed and processed for understanding.

HIERARCHICAL FOCUS

A hierarchical focus is the first principle in the establishment of an emphasis of visual elements that can draw and maintain the attention of the reader. Equally important are contrast, balance, and an ordering system that also provides the necessary mechanics that make one page layout superior to another. Furthermore, an over-dominance, either in quantity, intensity (boldness), or visual size of graphic elements (photographs, illustrations, etc.) can also forsake the mission of the designer to provide an appropriate balance of type and image that can attract and hold the attention of a sophisticated user of visual information.

The examples in Figure 8-3 show pages that progress from one block of type to a more dynamically balanced and focused page. The first page (A) is immediately translated by the eye and brain as a flat, neutral, gray mass with no focal point. This undefined mass provides no place where the eye can begin, conclude, and rest from its movement. Such page dullness created by solid type can only deter the designer from communicating the necessary information. The second and third pages (B and C) reveal an improved layout that includes both movement and focus

HIERARCHICAL FORM

The following example show a further development of the previous group. This set, however, shows more of an emphasis on typographic form that further hierarchically subdivides the page space by groups of information according to content. This form of grouping could also be considered a kind of basic cueing that further transforms the flat, monotonous field of information into discrete portions that are more quickly and easily accessed by the reader.

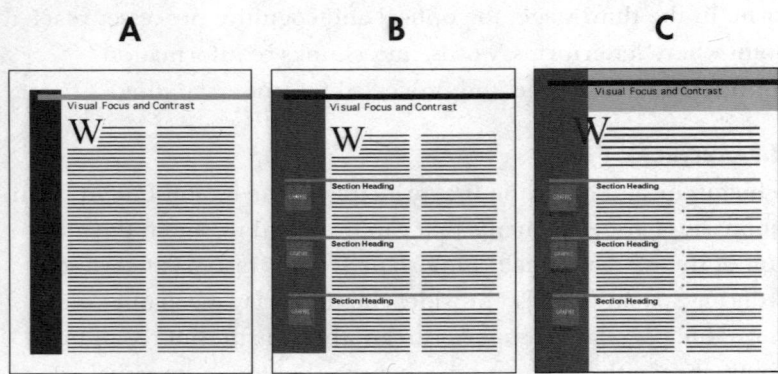

Figure 8-4. Illustration shows: A. Basic layout without elaboration. B. Further development of structuring information. C. Additional structure provides a further ability for the reader to focus.

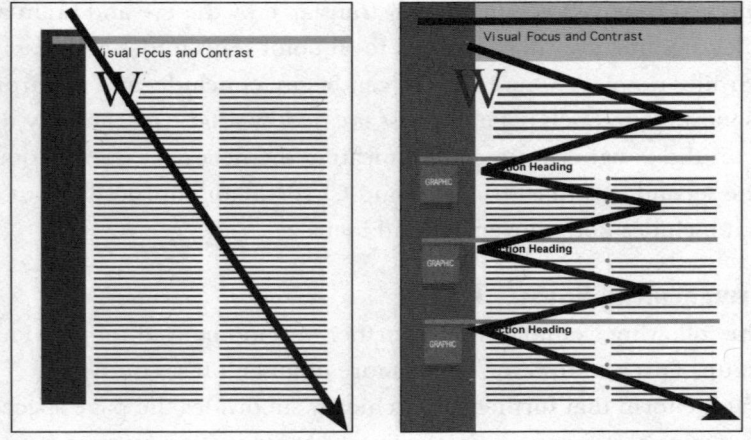

Figure 8-5. Illustration shows: A. Basic and simplest eye movement from top-left to bottom-right. B. More complex eye movement with a starting point, but also with multiple focus point that leads the eye through a path of information.

DIRECTING EYE MOVEMENT

In Western cultures, written materials are read from left to right and from the top of the page to the bottom. This basic visual orientation has been conditioned from childhood. Based on this, this axis should dominate the way a page layout should be constructed. In such a layout, the top or top left of the page is generally the dominant starting point from which the eye begins to travel across a page. Eye movement can go from top left to bottom right in a simple design or begin in the top-most location and zigzag in a downward direction moving to the bottom left corner.

It is possible for the designer to use both layout and typographic attributes to direct and even manipulate the order in which information is perceived by the reader. The skill needed to guide the reader from area to area on any given page is part of the knowledge of visual science that is necessary and useful in the art of typographic communication.

9 TYPE AND COLOR

Although the eye can perceive millions of colors, the designer
should be selective in applying color to type. This is because color
is another form of information that the brain must process and
understand relative to the overall depiction and arrangement of
visual elements. Seasoned designers skillfully use color with type or
type that has color to generate a sense of unity, consistency, or sensation that relates the content of the text.

The use of colored type in conjunction with illustrations or
photographs adds another dimension to any graphic product. This
is especially true when applied in textual cueing, e.g., to function
as a signal of change related to content. By using the primary colors
red, blue, and yellow or the secondary colors orange, violet, and
green with variations of tints or shapes, the designer can utilize
color coding, color cueing, or any combination of color interac-
tions that can improve the readability of type. If, however, these
devices are used improperly or inadequately, they can detract or
severely deter the designer from reaching the goal of typographic
clarity.

Before we address some of the key topics of type and color, a
brief overview of color theory will provide the background knowledge necessary to have a better understanding of this subject.

COLOR THEORY

BACKGROUND

In 1666 Sir Isaac Newton proved for the first time that color was
light itself and that the colors we see are reflected light. All visible

color is contained in the electromagnetic spectrum (band) of energy. When the entire band is present, it is perceived as white. When a portion of that band exists, it is because an object has absorbed most of the other colors in the spectrum and has reflected only its color. When white light passes through a prism, it bends and separates according to its wavelengths and we see color. In the visual arts we consider white to be the absence of all color. In this way white becomes the designer's background or palette onto which color is applied.

To understand how color is applied, it is important first to understand a variety of terms.

SUBTRACTIVE AND ADDITIVE COLOR

Subtractive color uses paints, dyes, inks, and natural pigments or colorants to create color. A colorant that absorbs one wavelength band has the combined color of the other two; it is the complement of the color it subtracts from white light.

Additive color is the method of creating color by blending two or three colors of light. These primary colors are commonly red, green, and blue (RGB). A key feature of additive color is that it deals with the color effects of light rather than pigments or dyes. An example of additive color is the color television screen or RGB monitor.

COLOR DIMENSIONS

The three dimensions of color are hue (color), chroma (saturation), and value (tone). *Hue* refers to the name of a color relative to other colors in the color spectrum. It is the qualitative variation of color. *Chroma* is the degree of brightness or dullness of a color. It is the quantitative variation of color in degree of intensity or purity because of the saturation of pigment. *Value* is the degree of lightness or darkness of color, in other words, the degree of tint or shade.

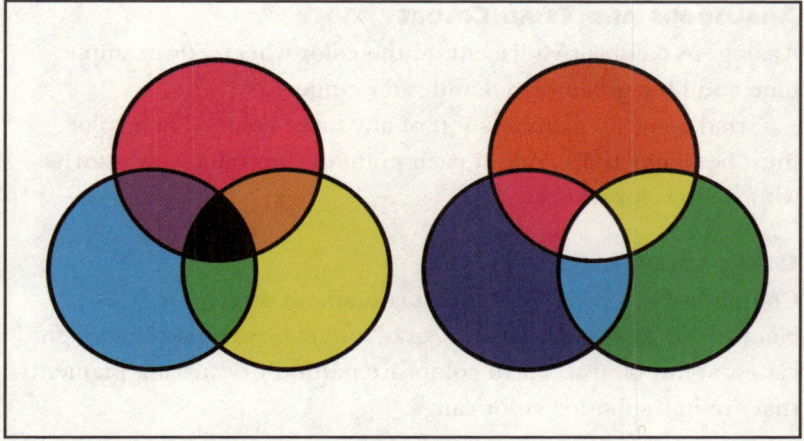

Figure 9-1. Illustration of subtractive and additive colors.

PRIMARY AND SECONDARY COLORS

Traditionally, primary colors are considered to be red, yellow, and blue. In printing, the primary colors are magenta, yellow, and cyan. Hues are considered as absolute or completely pure because they cannot be derived from the mixture of any other colors.

Secondary colors are orange, green, and violet (purple). These colors are made from a mixture of two primary colors. Their hue is midway between the two primaries.

TERTIARY AND MONOCHROMATIC COLOR

Tertiary or intermediate colors are orange red, yellow orange, yellow green, blue green, blue violet, and red violet. This group of colors includes any mixture of a primary and secondary color.

Monochromatic color harmony is by far the most basic, being a range of value and intensity of only one color.

COMPLEMENTARY AND SPLIT-COMPLEMENT COLORS

Complementary colors are directly across from one another on the color wheel. For example, red and green or yellow and violet.

Split-complement colors are found by first locating the complementary color and then finding the adjacent colors.

ANALOGOUS AND TRIAD COLORS

Analogous colors are adjacent on the color wheel. For example, blue and blue green or red and red orange.

Triad color is a combination of any three colors. Each color must be of equal distance at each point of the triangle as it turns within the color wheel.

OTHER COLOR FACTS

Compound colors are colors that contain all three primaries. Neutral colors are black, white, gray, and colors containing a significant amount of gray. Earth colors are naturally occurring pigments that are in a subdued color range.

COLOR AND USER PREFERENCE

Every color generates its own innate associated response based on the reader's preference, personality, and background. Throughout the world, the function, significance, and understanding of color varies depending on a reader's social, historical, and cultural perspective. How an American will respond to red may stimulate a different response from a Chinese or Brazilian person. The use of earth tones like brown and amber may conjure up one feeling in the U.S. but another in Japan or Korea. Objectively certain colors can convey a certain feeling and can be used as tools to make a statement in advertising, information graphics, or a number of products we see in the market today.

The effective application of color with type should be both objective and subjective. Even within the same culture, every person has a different perception of color based on a broad array of variables. What may be a true red to one person could be different to another. These differences are based on preconditioned cognitive responses that dictate what has been designated as red in prior interaction with the same or similar color.

Other conditions that affect these differences can also include various degrees of colorblindness or other optical disorders or the environment in which the color is being seen. These environments can vary according to the lighting conditions and nearby objects that are reflecting other colors, textures, and surrounding surfaces.

In addition to the typographic factors mentioned previously, color also contributes to a reader's confidence and understanding of the type they read. Color adds real soul to type because it strikes the chord of human emotions. Color in type has also been used for identification and distinction, i.e., to designate rank or status. Symbolically it has been used to evoke danger, peace, love, and death. Color theory is not the aim of this book, but it is important to recognize that the use of colored type brings another dimension to the creation of typographic design.

FACTORS FOR SELECTING COLOR FOR TYPE

KNOWLEDGE, EXPERIENCE, AND INSIGHT: FOUNDATION STONES FOR COLOR SELECTION

Selecting color for type should be guided by three prime factors: knowledge, experience, and insight. Color cannot be introduced merely for color's sake but to achieve a specific purpose. For this the designer should first have a basic knowledge and understanding of type and color theory. This includes the principles of good typography related to typefaces and the full range of attributes. If a designer does not understand the concept of readability combined with the effects of certain color combinations, the quality of the resulting design will be questionable. Second, experience is always the best teacher to perfect one's decisions and judgment. Third, insight can only come as a result of acquiring the adequate knowledge and experience obtained through years of working with type and color. From this, intuition and visual sensitivity provide a deeper aptitude for the use of color and typography.

BASIC COLOR SELECTION GUIDELINES

The first principle of color selection is to acknowledge that high contrasts are difficult to achieve with color combinations other than black and white. Printed materials are most readable in black and white. Nevertheless, different colors may be important for aesthetic or other reasons, but it is better to use such combinations only for larger or highlighted text, such as headlines and titles.

To achieve an effective level of visual clarity of type and color it is important to keep in mind these general guidelines:

- Exaggerate contrast between foreground and background colors.
- Avoid using colors of similar lightness adjacent to one another, even if they differ in saturation or hue.
- Choose dark colors against light colors.
- Avoid contrasting light colors from the bottom half against dark colors from the top half.
- Avoid complementary colors from adjacent parts of the color wheel.

COLOR CODING

Color research has provided a larger spectrum of user associations and responses to color and color combinations. Because the designer is intimately involved in the decision-making process of color selections, he or she should avoid an oversimplified under- standing of the effects of color coding text. Research consistently suggests that the use of color-coding to highlight particular words and sentences requires special attention. The regulated testing of such techniques is necessary to assure optimum legibility and func- tionality. Examples of such research in print and display legibility can be seen in the testing of visual search time on color-coded information displays.

The designer must be aware of the variables in color usage and should experiment with numerous combinations of hue, value, and chroma before confirming his or her choice, reserving the option for later changes. Then, after preliminary color choices are made, test the tentative selections on trial users for immediate feedback to ascertain legibility, readability, coding denotations, color functionality, balance, and overall usability and friendliness.

The following are some key suggestions for selecting color with type.

- **Use commonplace denotations in color selections for coding particular action-related cues.** For example, red for danger, stop, caution, warning; yellow for yield, pause, consider, wait for a moment before going on; green for go, go to next page or screen, proceed, okay, all clear.

- **Based on the limited color memory of some users, as well as colorblindness, color-coded items should have distinct hue, value, and chroma differences.** Color in combination with iconic images can provide a more accurate coding of access devices and cueing.

- **Consistency in color coding is crucial.** If one color is designated with one associated meaning or action, maintain that system of denotation. Redundancy in coding can only improve visual communication of information. This is especially true in training the user to the variety of visual cues and access devices for smooth mobility through any instructional system.

- **Selecting discrete words, headings, or phrases in a color helps readers quickly retrieve specific material of interest.** If you carry the variable color scheme through to other sections or your color-coding categorization scheme is not obvious, you may need to code it to a key.

10 DIGITAL TYPE

The evolution of typography, typesetting, and digital font creation has undergone many changes since the 1980s. As a result, it is impossible to cover all of the technical details in this volume. Related to typography, there have been five major innovations that have drastically changed electronic or desktop publishing since this time.

These developments include the Bézier curve, PostScript, TrueType, Multiple Masters, and type management. All of these technologies point us to a trend for more user control over the visual look and output of type. Following is a brief explanation of these key aspects in digital typography today.

THE BÉZIER CURVE

Pierre Bézier (pronounced *Bez'-e-a*) is a French engineer and scientist who, in the 1970s, developed a method of describing any line by specifying certain points along that same line and providing handles that could control the segments between the points. In essence, the Bézier curve is a simple cubic equation that can be used in a variety of ways.

Although the Bézier curve was initially invented for computer-aided design/manufacturing, this was a tremendous breakthrough for the digital typography industry. With this new technique of line rendering, any shape could be defined with just a few points, being far, far fewer than the number of dots that a bitmap representation requires to make the exact same curve.

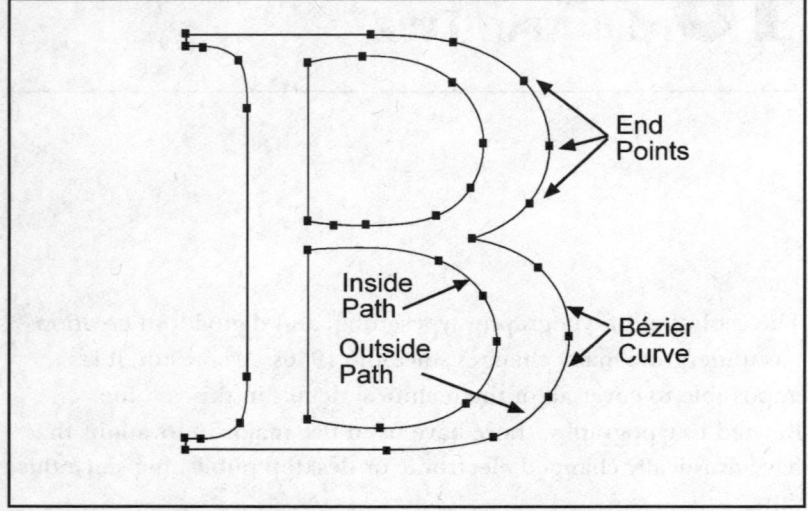

End Points

Inside Path

Outside Path

Bézier Curve

Figure 10-1. This illustration shows an uppercase B that has been rendered with thirty-seven Bézier curves with three paths.

The Bézier curve has become the foundation of Adobe's PostScript rendering capacity. For any professional involved in graphics it is sure to be used in such programs as Adobe Illustrator, Macromedia FreeHand, Adobe PageMaker, Adobe InDesign, QuarkXPress, Fontographer, or any number of three-dimensional graphics programs, whether for static or animated images.

POSTSCRIPT TYPOGRAPHY

The introduction of PostScript into the marketplace was simultaneous with the first 300-dpi laser printers in the mid-1980s. Before the innovation of PostScript by Adobe Systems, the desktop generation of type was by way of a bitmapped output device called a matrix printer. Software programs that produced these type fonts worked with a raster image or grid array made up of pixels. This raster image, made up of thousands of pixels, was called a *bitmap*.

PostScript is a page description language that has the monumental power to output high-resolution typographic characters as vectors to a laser printer by making an outlined point-to-point array.

PostScript also has the ability to do this while being device independent, that is, regardless of the manufacturer of the printing device. Because the vector-based fonts are created from Bézier curves, they can be easily mathematically scaled either down or up proportionately to any given size. Today PostScript fonts still produce the highest quality output, and PostScript is the system of choice by most professional designers and typographers.

TRUETYPE TYPOGRAPHY

TrueType is a digital font format jointly developed by Apple Computer and Microsoft as an alternative to Adobe PostScript fonts. TrueType fonts are described to the computer as outlines, which have the ability to enlarge, reduce, or manipulate the shape according to the designer's specifications. TrueType fonts are an alternative to PostScript fonts, though technically the difference is slight. TrueType fonts are available for the Macintosh and Windows systems, but they are not interchangeable. TrueType eliminates the need to have both screen and printer font files, because both functions are built into one font file driver.

TrueType fonts are very popular in the office environment and have their place in multimedia authoring systems but have not had much success in attracting the overall design and publishing industry. There has always been a struggle in the design and printing communities between TrueType and PostScript users. PostScript fonts, however, have been able to maintain their dominance in the industry.

MULTIPLE MASTERS

Multiple Masters typefaces provide a dimension to typographic control with an unprecedented flexibility to the user. Most Adobe Type 1 fonts are available in a fixed set of variants, like Regular and Bold, but the technology behind Multiple Masters fonts allows the end user to manipulate the font in more than one dimension. Available for the Macintosh and Windows environments, it has the power to

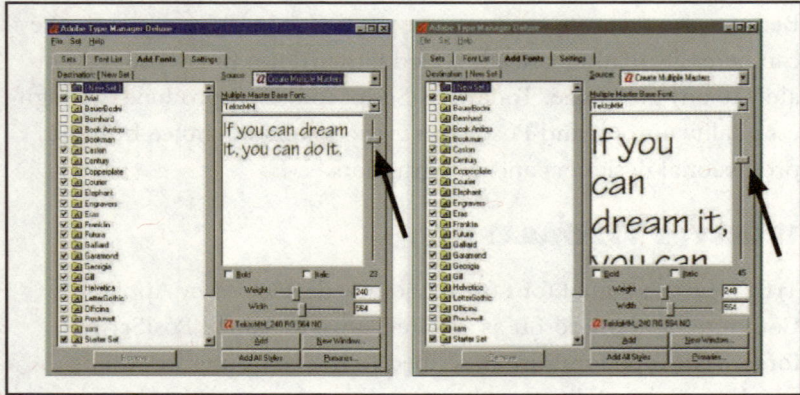

Figure 10-2. This illustration shows the Multiple Masters ability to rapidly modify type size. Notice the adjustable scale slider on the right.

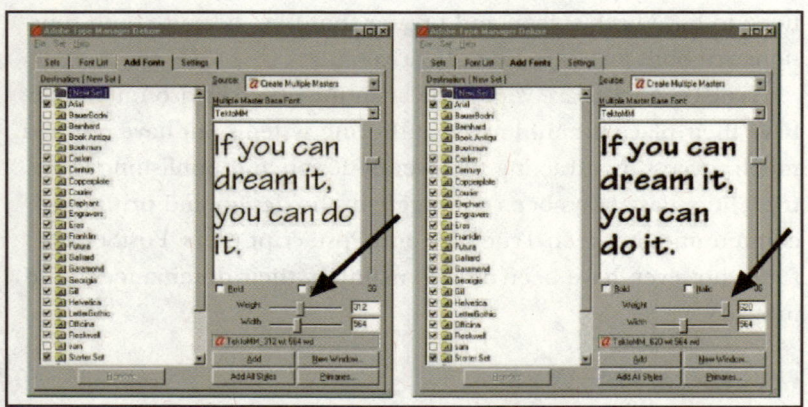

Figure 9-3. This illustration shows the Multiple Masters ability to rapidly modify type weight. Notice the adjustable weight slider under the viewing box on the top.

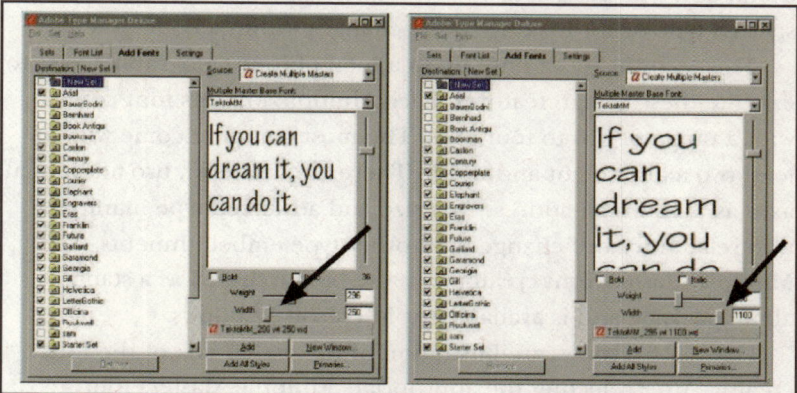

Figure 10-4. This illustration shows the Multiple Masters ability to rapidly modify type width. Notice the adjustable weight slider under the viewing box under the weight slider.

Type Type Type Type Type
Type Type Type Type Type
Type Type Type Type Type
Type Type Type Type Type

Figure 10-5. This illustration demonstrates the degree of flexibility of the Multiple Masters in creating a wide variety of letterforms from one typeface. Notice the variations of weight and width.

simultaneously create all potential typographical distortions. It is useful as a type-designing tool for creating new headlines or special stylized type or for making subtle changes within a body of text.

This technology can use up to a total of four typographic axes to execute these design features. Each Multiple Masters font comes with a range of two to four axes. The most common come with at least two axes: weight and width. There are, however, two additional axes as well, which address type size and advanced type manipulation related to serif changes and other type embellishments. The Multiple Masters font creator can also be purchased as a stand-alone package and is available for Microsoft Windows.

Figure 10-2 shows an illustration of the dialog box of the font creator. After selecting the appropriate Multiple Masters font desired, move the slide bar back and forth to achieve the desired effects, as shown on the small display window. After clicking *OK*, a new example or instance of the font will be created instantly and will appear in the font menu of your computer.

Besides the existing controls for changing the width or height of type, in some publishing and illustration software, Multiple Masters can allow the user to change these attributes while retaining the correct letterform proportions and stroke thickness. You can smoothly vary a Multiple Masters font along one or more design axes, giving rise to a number of letterform variants. The Multiple Masters fonts have one or more design axes, such as weight, width, optical size, and style.

Figures 10-3 and 10-4 show the basic concept using the TektoMM Multiple Master font, which has the capability of two design axes, weight and width. By moving the slide bars back and forth, the user is able to manipulate both axes. Figure 10-5 is a matrix, which shows the variations of width and height axis type manipulation while keeping their original intrinsic letterform characteristics.

TYPE MANAGEMENT

Type management has become a growing area of concern for designers and typographers using publishing systems. Printing or rendering problems generally occur independent of the output device, and, as a result, font files need specific management to curtail errors that may occur within the operating system. Besides specific computer computational errors, problems can be related to font substitution or the rendering of the type with an output device that has an inaccurate understanding of the digital information that it is receiving. Of course, this problem may be with the printer and not the actual font files that it is receiving.

ADOBE TYPE MANAGER AND ADOBE TYPE REUNION

Many issues related to font management have been addressed through publishing utilities like Adobe Type Manager and Adobe Type Reunion. Adobe Type Manager allows fonts to be used as screen fonts while being seen on the computer screen as they would be printed by the laser printer. Adobe Type Manager uses information in the printer fonts to scale screen fonts to whatever size needed when the designer is working.

Adobe Type Reunion is a valuable utility that groups font families together by displaying only the proper name of the font without all of the variations. For example, as you bring your cursor down the type list, the main name of the font will appear. When you stop and hold your cursor at that point, the related variations will appear.

CONCLUSION

The languages of the world have always found their way into the visible realm. As words became forms of visual communication across the boundaries of time, culture, and social rank, typography bore the responsibility of making the written word both attractive and effective. From the most primitive to the most modern, both art and technology have matured together to make the mechanical aspects of typography readily available to all. The task, however, is for the designer and users of typographic form to apply the knowledge that can still make this visual language dynamic yet useful in a practical manner to the reader.

It is the author's hope that this text provided the beginner the elementary knowledge that could make a difference as he or she brings his or her typographic skills into a world where information overload bombards the reader at every turn. Hence, for this cause the *Typography Primer* was written.

GLOSSARY

AGATE Body type measuring approximately 5½ points. The agate is frequently used to specify the depth of newspaper advertising. Fourteen agate lines are equivalent to one column inch.

ALIGNMENT (1) The horizontal positioning of characters. In base alignment, characters rest on a common horizontal line, excluding descenders and irrespective of aesthetics and design proportions. (2) In typesetting, alignment denotes the exact (even) relationship at the top (or bottom) of the letters in a font. The term can also refer to setting lines of type so that the ends appear even. See also: *justification*.

ALLEY The spaces between tabular copy. It is occasionally referred to as column margins or columns. See also: *gutter*.

ALPHABET LENGTH The space required for letters of a given font expressed in points, or the length of the lowercase alphabet of a particular type font.

ANTIQUA Synonymous with the word *serif*.

APEX The upper point of letters with an ascending pointed form; the point usually extends past the cap line.

ARC Sometimes used to describe the part of the boundary of a letterform that is elliptical in appearance; also referred to as the *shoulder*.

AREA COMPOSITION Preparing data for typesetting in such form that all or as many elements of the final page as possible are typeset in place. This reduces or eliminates pasteup. Area composition output falls somewhere between galley output (requiring extensive pasteup) and full page makeup with all elements in place.

ARM The horizontal or diagonal upward sloping stroke that is free on one end and attaches to the stem.

ASCENDER The portion of a lowercase character that extends above the height of the main body of the character. Some examples include *h, k, l, b*, and *d*. See also: *descender*.

ASYMMETRY Aspects of letterforms that reflect the mirror image relationship between letter pairs (e.g., *bd* and *pq*) or in a single letter (*T*).

AUTOKERNING The automatic reduction of unwanted white space between type characters.

AXIS The real or imaginary straight line on which a letterform rotates or appears to turn.

BACK MARGIN The distance between the fold edge and the edge of the body of the type (text matter) next to the fold. Alternative terms: *binding margin, gutter margin*.

BAD BREAK In text composition, setting a hyphenated line as the first line of a page; ending a page with the first line of a paragraph or a single word or hyphenated word; or dividing a word incorrectly anywhere in the text.

BARBS The half serifs at the ends of the arcs of letters like *C, G,* and *S,* as seen in the Old Style typefaces.

BASE ALIGNMENT Positioning different typefaces and sizes with their characters all on the same optical baseline. See also: *baseline.*

BASELINE A typographic term for defining the imaginary line on which the bottom serifs of lowercase letters such as *x, w,* and *m* seem to rest.

BEARD In hot-metal typesetting, the beveled space below the printing surface of a type letter.

BEZIER CURVE A vector graphic, named after Pierre Bezier, that is defined mathematically by two endpoints and two or more other points that control its shape.

BIND MARGIN The gutter or inner margin of a book, from the binding to the printed area.

BLOCK LETTERS Type cut from wood, or type that resembles letters cut from wood (Gothic or sans serif letters).

BODY The size of type from the top of the ascenders to the bottom of the descenders.

BODY COPY The textual matter usually set in one face and point size with a common leading and column width.

BODY SIZE A hot-metal typography term denoting the measurement from the top to the bottom of a piece of type. In phototypesetting, the body size is identical to the point size of the character.

BODY TYPE Text set in paragraph or block form, as distinguished from heads and display type matter. Alternative term: *body matter.*

BOLDFACE TYPE A version of a typeface that is heavier than the normal weight

in the type family. Boldface type is used for emphasis.

BOWL The curved stroke that makes an enclosed space within a character. In an open bowl, the stroke does not meet with the stem completely, e.g. in uppercase type *C, G, O,* and in lowercase type *b, c, e.*

BRACKETED SERIF A serif in which the transition from the stem to the serif stroke is one continuous smooth curve.

CALIFORNIA JOB CASE An open box with compartments in which individual type characters are separated for the hand compositor.

CALLIGRAPHY Various styles of elegant handwriting, many based on classic examples from the fourteenth through the eighteenth centuries.

CALLOUT A selection of type, usually a word or phrase, that is set apart on the page, and is larger and/or bolder type from the body-copy font for emphasis.

CAP HEIGHT The height of a capital letter from the baseline to the top of the letter in a particular typeface.

CAPITAL The larger letters of the alphabet and which was the original form of ancient Roman Latin characters; also referred to as *uppercase, majuscule,* or *all-caps.*

CAPS Capital or uppercase letters.

CAPS, SMALL A second size of uppercase letters made on the same body size as regular capital letters. Small caps are usually close in size to the lowercase characters in the font.

CASE Traditionally upper- and lowercase referred to when lead type was stored in a printer's printing case, but today, case refers to the capitalization or noncapitalization of letters in a word.

CENTERED A typographic form in which various line lengths of type are symmetrically divided by a common vertical axis. The longest line of type represents the line length.

CHARACTER COMPENSATION Reducing the width value of each printed symbol, which, in turn, decreases the white space between characters for tighter fit. See also: *kerning*.

CHARACTER SET The particular array of character designs available on a typesetter, word processor and printer, or typewriter. Alternative term: *type font*.

CHARACTER WIDTH SYSTEMS The amount of horizontal space a character occupies in relation to adjacent characters.

CHROMA A term used in the Munsell system of color specification to indicate the extent to which the color is diluted by white light. The intensity or strength of a color. Its saturation or degree of departure from black and white.

CICERO The continental typographic measure equivalent to 12 points Didot, or 4.511 mm. See also: *Didot point system*.

COLD TYPE Characters produced on paper or film for photomechanical reproduction without the use of metal type. The term originally applied to any method of preparing text by direct-impression from typewriter mechanisms. Today, it usually refers to phototypeset galleys, laser-printed proofs, or paginated films generated from imagesetters.

COLOR A visual sensation produced in the brain when the eye views various wavelengths of light. Color viewing is a highly subjective experience that varies from individual to individual. In the graphic arts industry, lighting standards and color charts help ensure the accuracy of color reproduction.

COLOR CAST Modifying a hue by adding a trace of another hue to create such combinations as yellowish green or pinkish blue. Color casts can be undesirable as in the contamination of the desired hue by a second hue. For example, a gray intended to appear as a neutral can under some conditions have a red, yellow, or blue cast or appearance. Other colors can have a cast as well, e.g., reds with a yellow or blue cast or blues with a red or yellow cast, etc.

COLOR PRIMARIES, ADDITIVE The three basic colors, which, when properly selected and mixed, produce any hue. In the visual spectrum, the three primary colors are green, red, and blue. When combined, these colors form white light. In the printing process, the three primary (process) colors are yellow, magenta, and cyan.

COLUMN A vertical arrangement of text characters, numbers, or other symbols.

COLUMN INCH A unit of measurement that is one inch deep and one column wide.

COLUMN RULE A line used to separate vertical arrangements of text in printed matter.

COMPLEMENTARY COLORS Any two opposite (or contrasting) colors that produce white or gray when combined. In printing, complementary colors neutralize or accentuate each other, diminishing or enhancing the attention value of the print.

COMPOSE Setting text in the proper order and form.

COMPOSING The process of setting type.

COMPOSING MACHINES Typesetting machines used to cast and compose type in justified lines. Intertype, Linotype, and Monotype machines are some examples.

COMPOSING ROOM. The area in a printing plant where type is set.

COMPOSING STICK With movable type, a small, hand-held tray where type is assembled and justified after it is hand-selected from the type case. Alternative term: *job stick; stick*.

COMPOSITION (1) Setting or assembling type. (2) Formatting typeset text before printing. Alternative terms: *pagination and page makeup*. See also: *phototypesetting; typesetting*.

COMPOSITOR A person who sets type.

CONDENSED A typeface in which the height is proportionally greater than its width. A visually compressed font, with less than a normal appearance; usually a condensed face is much taller than it is wide.

COPY Any material given to the printer for reproduction, particularly text and artwork. Alternative term: *original*.

COPYFITTING Adjusting copy to the allotted space, by editing the text or changing the type size and leading.

COUNTER The white space enclosed by a letterform, whether wholly enclosed or partially, e.g., as seen with *d* or *o* or with *c* or *m*.

CROSS STROKE The horizontal bar connecting two strokes of a letter, e.g., in the letters *H, T,* or *A*.

CURSIVE Typefaces that resemble handwriting or script that usually join between letters.

CYAN A blue-green color, complementary to red. Along with yellow and magenta, one of the three primary subtractive colors or process colors used in the printing process. Cyan reflects blue and green light, while absorbing red.

DASH A typographical character or sign. Dashes are classified according to the following four criteria: weight, design, width of image and allotted space, and vertical position. Some examples include the em and en dashes.

DESCENDER The portion of a lowercase type character that extends below the common baseline of a typeface design, such as in *g, j, p, q,* and *y*. See also: *ascender*.

DIDOT POINT SYSTEM A European method of printing measurement. Twelve didot points equal the didot pica or cicero. The didot point is equal to 0.0148 inch; the cicero is 0.1776 inch.

DIFFERENTIAL LETTERSPACING See *spacing, proportional*.

DIGITAL TYPE Characters composed of dots.

DIGITAL TYPOGRAPHY The use of computers for design, engineering, or presenting type under digital control.

DINGBAT Symbols that are not a part of any particular typeface but are a range of symbols and/signs.

DIPHTHONG Combining two characters into a single graphic and single sound, such as "æ" and "œ" in words of Greek origin.

DISPLAY TYPE Those type styles and sizes designed mainly for use as headline and advertising matter, instead of as straight text or body composition. Alternative term: *display matter*.

DOUBLE COLUMN A page consisting of two vertical sections of printed type separated by a rule or blank space.

DROP CAP This is a large initial capital in the beginning of a paragraph that extends through several lines.

DROP FOLIO A page number that is dropped to the foot of the page and is often used on chapter openings. See folio, drop and footer.

DROP INITIAL Typographic style in which an oversize initial is placed so as to "drop" below the top alignment of the accompanying text setting.

DUMMY (1) A preliminary layout showing the position of illustrations, text, folds, and other design elements as they are to appear in the printed piece. (2) A diagram of each newspaper page, prepared by the editorial department, to guide compositors in placing and fitting stories and illustrations.

EAR The small stroke projecting from the top of lowercase, e.g., *r, f,* or *a.*

ELECTRONIC COMPOSITION Computer-assisted methods of copyfitting and pagination that output text and graphical elements in completed page form as paper galleys or film from an imagesetter.

EM A printer's unit of area measurement equal in width and height to the height of the letter *M* in any selected type body size. Now commonly used as an abbreviation of pica-em, where the em is equivalent to 12 points (approximately one-sixth inch). See also: *en.*

EM DASH A line one em long that connects interrelated or parenthetical material in typeset text. Alternative term: *long dash, mutt dash.*

EM SPACE A nonprinting fixed space equal in width to the point size of a font. It is used for indenting paragraphs and aligning type columns. Alternative term: *em quad.* See also: *en space; thin space.*

EN A printer's unit of area measurement equal to the same height but half the width of the em. The en is sometimes used to specify the area of composition as its value closely approximates the number of characters in the text. See also: *em.*

EN DASH A line one en long that connects interrelated material in typeset text.

EN QUAD A nonprinting fixed typographic space that is one-half the em space; the width of an arabic numeral if the font does not contain a special figure space.

EN SPACE A blank space half the value of the em space; usually equal to the width of a numeral in text sizes. It is used for

alignment of figure columns and indentions. See also: *em space.*

EXTENDED OR EXPANDED A type design variation with more than normal width settings, i.e., type that appears to have been stretched from left to right; is wide in appearance; or is an extended font that is wider than the corresponding regular font.

EXTENDER The parts of the letterform that extend below the baseline, e.g., *p, q.*

EYE The counter (enclosed) area at the top of the lowercase *e.*

FACE See *typeface.*

FACING PAGES In a double-sided publication, the two pages that face (facing-pages) each other when the publication is open.

FAMILY The variations of typefaces within the same design pattern that have similar characteristics of serifs, strokes, proportion, and balance within a particular species of type, such as Times Roman, Times Italic, Times Bold, etc.

FEET The base of a piece of metal type.

FIT A term used to describe the horizontal spacing or relationship between two or more characters. Fit can be altered by kerning or modifying the horizontal width (set width) assigned to characters. Evaluating fit is generally subjective.

FIXED SPACE A typographic unit with a constant width instead of a variable width. The em and en are examples of fixed spaces.

FLUSH Type composition set without paragraph indentions.

FLUSH LEFT Lines of type composition aligned to the left margin, with a ragged right margin. Alternative terms: *quadded left; ragged right; unjustified text.* See also: *justification.*

FLUSH RIGHT Lines of composition aligned to the right margin with a ragged left margin. Alternative terms: *quadded right; ragged left.* See also: *justification.*

FOLIO In printing, a page number, often placed at the outside of the running head, at the top (head) of the page. See also: *header.* (2) In descriptive bibliography, a leaf of a manuscript or early printed book, the two sides designated as *r* (recto, or front) and *v* (verso, or back).

FOLIO, DROP In printing, a page number, often placed at the outside of the running head at the bottom (foot) of the page. See also: *footer.*

FONT A complete collection of characters in one typeface and size, including all letters, figures, symbols, and punctuation marks. See also: *typefonts, "tuned."*

FOOT MARGIN The distance between the bottom edge of the body of type (text matter) on a page and the bottom edge of the trimmed page. Alternative term: *tail margin.*

FOOTER A book's title or a chapter title printed at the bottom of a page. A drop folio (page number) may or may not be included. Alternative term: *running foot.* See also: *folio, drop; header.*

FORMAT Size, shape, and design of a printed piece.

FOUNDRY TYPE Hand-set metal type characters.

GALLEY A typeset proof of text from the phototypesetting machine that is run out as one long column of type.

GOTHIC TYPE A plain sans serif typeface with lines of unvarying thickness.

GREEKED TEXT Simulated (fake) text used to represent type, e.g., the use of gray bars or "dummy" characters to represent text in a layout so that the design of the document will be emphasized rather than its content.

GRID In art and copy preparation, a preprinted, standardized format or template on a sheet of acetate or (in non-reproducible blue) on a pasteup board. The artist uses such grids as guidelines in the pasteup of a specific, and usually repeatable job, such as a magazine, where the format remains the same, but the content changes month after month.

GUTTER In typography, the inside margin (white space) between facing pages or columns of type. In bookbinding, the margin at the binding edge. Alternative terms: *gutter margin; back margin.* See also: *alley.*

HAIRLINE The secondary stroke of a letter, usually thinner than the stem.

HAND COMPOSITION Method of setting type manually from a case with a composing stick.

HANGING INDENT Typesetting the first line of a paragraph to the full text width, while succeeding lines are spaced in by a constant amount from the left margin.

HANGING PUNCTUATION Commas, hyphens, etc., set outside the normal line length on the left- and right-hand sides of the column of type to achieve optical alignment or a certain aesthetic appearance.

HEAD A line of display type signifying the title of a work or conveying crucial information. A headline.

HEAD MARGIN. The distance between the top edge of the trimmed page and the top edge of the body of type (text matter) on a page.

HEADER A book's title or a chapter title printed at the top of a page and often with a folio (page number). Alternative term: *running head.* See also: *folio; footer.*

HOT TYPE The general term for type, which is cast from hot molten metal.

HUE A visual property determined by the dominant light wavelengths reflected or transmitted.

HYPHENATION The division of a typeset word between syllables at the end of a line.

HYPHENLESS JUSTIFICATION The alignment of lines of type through the use of interword and letter spacing instead of end-of-line word hyphenation.

IDEOGRAM A picture or symbol used in a system of writing to represent an idea.

IMAGESETTER A device used to output fully paginated text and graphic images at a high resolution onto photographic film, paper, or plates. See also: *typesetting, digital.*

INCUNABULA Early printing, specifically that done during the fifteenth century.

INDENT Setting type so that a portion of it aligns at a predetermined distance from the left or right margin of the column.

INFERIOR CHARACTER A letter and/or number positioned below the baseline of type and set in a smaller face. Alternative term: *subscript.* See also: *superior character.*

INITIAL LETTER A large capital or otherwise decorated character that begins a chapter or paragraph. Alternative term: *initial capital.*

INTERLINE SPACING See *leading.* Alternative term: *line spacing.*

ITALIC A slanted version of a typeface with vertical lines that are between 8° and 20° from the perpendicular to the character baseline. In typeset copy, italic type is used to signify periodical titles and other special information. See also: *oblique.*

ITC International Typeface corporation, a major vendor of typefaces.

JOB STICK See *composing stick.*

JUSTIFICATION The process of composing a line of type by spacing between the words and characters to fill an exact measure, thus aligning the type at both margins. Hyphenation is sometimes employed to achieve justification. In other cases, only the spacing between words is adjusted. See also: *alignment; flush right; flush left; ragged; word spacing.*

JUSTIFICATION, VERTICAL (1) The use of variable spacing between lines, or type elements, vertically in order to fill out a desired column or page depth. (2) Modifying point size and intercharacter spacing instead of vertical spaces in order to force a given block of type to fill a desired depth.

KERNING Manipulating type character widths and white space to achieve aesthetically pleasing results. Alternative term: *mortise.* See also: *spacing; word spacing.*

LASER TYPESETTING A technique whereby the light source directly imprints images onto paper or film.

LEADING The amount of space between the baseline of one line of type and the baseline of the adjacent line. The space is inserted to separate the type characters on the two lines. Alternative terms: *interline spacing; line spacing.*

LEADING, ADDITIONAL Space inserted between lines of type to supplement normal interline (between lines) leading. It is used to make the text aesthetically pleasing, more readable, or fit better in a defined area.

LEADING, NEGATIVE Type set with less space from baseline to baseline than the size of the type itself. Alternative term: *minus leading.*

LEADING, PRIMARY The prevailing leading between the lines of a piece of typeset text, excluding variations used between elements such as subheads or paragraphs.

LEADING, REVERSE The ability of a photo-typesetter to move back up a column or page in a specified amount. Reverse leading is often useful for setting multi-column work, fractions, and inferior and superior characters.

LEADING, SECONDARY (1) An alternate leading value used repeatedly between particular elements such as subheads or paragraphs. (2) In some phototypeset-ting systems, an alternate value that is used to film advance an individual line upon command.

LEAF (1) A separate, usually blank, sheet of paper in a book. (2) A pigmented stamping material used to decorate book edges.

LEFT JUSTIFIED Setting text against the left margin, i.e., with unused space all placed at the right; and also called ragged right.

LEGIBILITY The ease with which text is read in ordinary, continuous reading, usually gauged by reading speed and error rate. Legibility concerns the read-er's ability to successfully find, identify, discriminate, and absorb the text. (A. Marcus, *Graphic Design for Electronic Documents and User Interfaces.)*

LETTER A graphic, which, when used alone or combined with others repre-sents in a written language one or more sound elements of the spoken language. Diacritical marks used alone and punc-tuation marks are not letters.

LETTER, PRIMARY A lowercase letter such as *e, m, n, o,* or *c* that does not have ascenders or descenders.

LETTERFORM A single glyph or letter shape.

LETTERSPACE To add space between the characters of a word or group of words, either for emphasis, or for aesthetic purposes when justifying short lines in a body of composition.

LIGATURE Two or more characters that are specially modified in design to be cast or exposed together as one unit, frequently with connecting strokes. Some examples include "fi" and "fl."

LIGHT FACE A term used to describe body text, which is usually set in type that is less bold than the Roman typeface in the same family and size.

LINE LENGTH The width to which a justi-fied line of type is set. Line length is usually expressed in points and picas in the U.S. or in didots and ciceros in Europe. Alternative term: *line measure.*

LINE SPACING See *leading.*

LINOTYPE Originally a hot metal typeset-ting system invented by Ottmar Mergenthaler in 1886 that utilized a key-board and sets one line of type at a time as a solid piece of lead.

LITHO STONE A natural homogeneous limestone originally employed as the chief printing surface in lithography. Some fine artists still create images with litho stones.

LITHOGRAPHY A printing process in which the image carrier is chemically treated so that the nonimage areas are receptive to water (i.e., dampening or fountain solution) and repel ink while the image areas are receptive to ink and repel water. The image carrier is said to be planographic, or flat and smooth.

LOOP The lower portion of the Roman lowercase *g* added as a flourish rather than an essential part of the letter.

LOOSE LINE A line of type in which inter-word spacing is excessive. A pattern or river of white space is often visible in a paragraph with a significant number of loose lines.

LOWERCASE The uncapitalized letters of the alphabet; originated from the semi-uncial lettering style, which evolved from the Caroline minuscules of approx-imately A.D. 800. Originally called lowercase because the lead type version was located in the lower portion of the type case. Alternative term: *minuscules*. See also: *uppercase*.

MAJUSCULE The capital letterform, e.g., *A, B, C,* etc.; also uppercase.

MARGIN The white space extending from the edge of the printed image to a page's trim edge.

MEASURE The length of a typeset line, expressed in picas.

MONOTONE OR MONOLINE TYPEFACE A font in which all the lines appear to be of the same thickness.

MOVABLE TYPE The individual metal or wooden type characters that are taken from the typecase, arranged to form words and sentences, and then returned to the case for reuse later.

OBLIQUE A simulated italic character produced electronically from standard Roman fonts.

OBLIQUING Electronically slanting characters by distorting an upright typeface so that each character is properly seated on the horizontal baseline while its upright axis deviates somewhat from the vertical in a forward or backward direction.

OLDSTYLE TYPE Roman typefaces that are based on earlier hand-drawn characters and distinguished in design from modern typefaces by their clear, strong features; the comparative uniform thickness of all strokes; the absence of hairlines; the irregularities among individual letters; and the diagonal serifs, curves, and cross-strokes.

OPEN A word used to characterize the visual appearance of typographic matter that is widely spaced or surrounded by large amounts of white space. This effect is used to avoid the dense, block-like appearance of solid masses of type.

ORPHAN The first line of a paragraph that is also the last line on a page or column, generally considered poor typography. Sometimes, the last line of a paragraph which is also the first line on a page is referred to as an orphan. See also: *widow*.

OVERSET Typeset characters exceeding the individual line length desired, usually unintentional.

OVERSTRIKE Superimposing one type character over another to correct copy. This method may be used instead of the insert and delete functions.

PAGINATION Laying out the parts of a document into pages, with a numbering system of pages in consecutive order.

PHOTOTYPESETTING A term for photographically produced type or cold type. The act of composing type and reproducing it on photographic film or paper.

PAPYRUS A tall plant native to the Nile region, the pith of which was sliced and pressed into matted sheets by the early Egyptians to produce the first writing material with many of the properties of paper. The word *paper* originated from papyrus.

PARCHMENT A fine, translucent paper made from the tanned hide of a sheep or goat.

PICA A printer's unit of linear measure, equal to approximately one-sixth of an inch. There are twelve points in a pica and approximately six picas in an inch.

PITCH (1) The number of characters per inch to be printed. The larger the number, the smaller the size of the print. (2) A unit of width of type, based on the number of characters that can be placed in a linear inch; for example, 10-pitch type has ten characters per inch.

PLATEN In letterpress, a movable flat surface that is pressed firmly against paper and inked type to produce a printed image.

Platen press A printing press with a flat printing surface and a flat impression surface.

Point (1) The smallest American unit of typographic linear measurement, equal to 0.0138 in. Type height is measured in points. (2) An alternative term for the punctuation mark called a "period."

Point size Specifying the height of the body of a typeface in units of linear measure equal to 0.0138 in. Alternative term: *type size.*

Point system The system of measuring by points and picas in typographic composition. It has been in use since 1878.

Punch The cutting of a letter of the alphabet at the end of a steel bar so that it can be punched into a brass mould or matrix from which to cast lead type.

Quad A blank piece of metal used in handset type to create the space between words. The term is also used to refer to spacing and alignment in phototypesetting.

Quad left A command code in a phototypesetter that instructs the machine to position all text to the left end of the line. A minimum of interword spacing and letterspacing is used in the portion of the line containing characters, and the right portion contains only space. Alternative term: *flush left; unjustified text.* See also: *quad right; tabular material.*

Quad right A command code in a phototypesetter that instructs the machine to position all text to the right end of the line. A minimum of interword spacing and letterspacing is used in the portion of the line containing characters, and the left portion contains only space. Alternative term: *flush right.* See also: *quad left; tabular material.*

Ragged Type composition set with lines centered in the column, instead of justified, producing raggedness at both sides. See also: *justification.*

Ragged left See *flush right.*

Ragged right See *flush left.*

Readability The speed or ease at which continuous text can be read based on the column width to point size ratio, the x-height of the font, the leading, the color of type, and the color of page.

Recto The right-hand page of an open book, usually an odd-numbered page; sometimes the first or cover page. See also: *verso.*

River The undesirable alignment of interword spaces in successive lines of type, which forms a pattern of white space that flows throughout the typeset material. See also: *underset.*

Roman type A term used to describe a regular serif or sans serif face that is neither italic nor bold. Roman typefaces are typically used in books.

Rule A printed line, usually specified by its arrangement and thickness or "weight," such as hairline, 2-point, 6-point, or parallel.

Runaround Setting text in a form to fit around an illustration or figure when the illustration is less than the column or page width.

Running foot See *footer; folio, drop.*

Running head See *header; folio.*

Sans serif Typeface designs, such as Helvetica, that lack the small extensions on the ascenders and descenders referred to as serifs. See also: *serif.*

Script A typeface that resembles cursive handwriting.

Secondary colors Colors that are produced by overprinting pairs of the primary subtractive colors. The subtractive secondary colors are red, green, and blue. Alternative term: *overprint colors.*

SERIF The short, usually perpendicular line found at the end of the unconnected or finishing stroke of a character. Serifs may vary in weight, length, and shape, and contribute greatly to the style of the typeface. See also: *sans serif.*

SERIF, SQUARE Typeface in which the serifs are the same weight or heavier than the main strokes.

SET WIDTH In composition, the normal space allowed across the body of each character along a line of set type. Alternative term: *set size.*

SHOULDER In hot-metal typography, the nonprinting top area of the type body that surrounds the character.

SLUG A complete line of type cast in a single piece of metal.

SPACING (1) In typography, justifying a line of type by inserting extra spacing between words. Letterspacing is adjusted to reduce the effects of excess justification. See also: *kerning; word spacing.* (2) In hot-metal typesetting, inserting leads or slugs to open up lines of composition.

SPACING, PROPORTIONAL A typesetting procedure in which additional spaces are placed between words so that a line of text can be fully justified.

SPACING, TRUE PROPORTIONAL A typesetting procedure in which character spacing is adjusted according to character width. For example, the letter *m* requires more width than the letter *i.*

SPECIFICATIONS A detailed description of the requirements for a job, the typography in particular. Alternative term: *"speccing."* See also: type *"speccing."*

SPUR The nodule that descends from the vertical stroke of an uppercase *G* connecting the straight stroke to the curved stroke.

STEM The primary vertical stroke of a type character.

STRESS The thickest point or maximum stress in a curved stroke caused by a flat pen changing direction.

STROKE Any part of a character that can be drawn with one movement.

SUBHEAD A secondary title or heading that is usually set in smaller type, making it less prominent than a main heading.

SUBSCRIPT See *inferior character.*

SUBTRACTIVE COLOR PROCESS A means of producing a color reproduction or image with combinations of yellow, magenta, and cyan colorants on a white substrate.

SUBTRACTIVE PRIMARIES The colors cyan, yellow, and magenta. Each is formed when one third of the spectrum is subtracted from white light. See also: *additive primaries.*

SUPERIOR CHARACTER A letter and/or number positioned above the x-height of a related word or character positioned on the baseline. Like inferior characters, superior characters are also set in a smaller typeface. Alternative term: *superscript.* See also: *inferior character.*

TAB See *tabular material; quad left; quad right.*

TABULAR MATERIAL Numeric and alphanumeric data set in parallel columns separated by blank spaces or divided by rules.

THIN SPACE A relative space of known value, usually one-fifth or one-quarter of an em space. See also: *em space.*

THUMB EDGE The outside edge of a book, directly opposite the binding edge.

TRIM MARGIN The white space on the open side of a signature.

TYPE The letters, numerals, and special figures produced in different faces and sizes by various composition methods.

TYPE FAMILY A set of typefaces derived from one basic design, e.g., the bold, italic, and condensed variations of the original face.

TYPE GAUGE A rule that is graduated in various point units and used to measure the body of type matter or the spacing between lines of type.

TYPE HIGH The height of a piece of type from its feet to its face. In the U.S. and Great Britain this measurement is standardized at 0.918 in.

TYPE SIZE See *point size*.

TYPE "SPECCING" Marking up a manuscript with the information required for typesetting. See also: *specifications*.

TYPE STYLES A system of general classifications for type, as distinguished by divisions such as Black Letter, Roman, Sans Serif, Script/Cursive, Italic, Decorative/Novelty, Glyphic, and Trash Type.

TYPEFACE A distinctive type design, usually produced in a range of sizes (fonts) and variations, including bold and italic.

TYPEFONT See *font*.

TYPEFONTS, "TUNED" Digital type images that are hand-edited to optimize the visual quality of the characters in relation to the resolution (lines per inch) of a given imaging technology, the actual resolution, the image spot energy profile, and the interaction between adjacent image spots.

TYPEFORM See *form*.

TYPESCRIPT A manuscript ready to be typeset.

TYPESET To compose type in a standardized form.

TYPESETTER (1) A machine that composes type according to certain standardized specifications. (2) The person who sets type. See also: *phototypesetter*.

TYPESETTER, FOURTH-GENERATION See *imagesetter*.

TYPESETTING Composing type into words and lines in accordance with the manuscript and typographic specifications. See also: *composition; phototypesetting*.

TYPESETTING, DIGITAL Imagesetters and third-generation phototypesetting machines that eliminate the need for film fonts by storing digital codes in the computer unit and producing type characters as microscopic dots. See also: *imagesetter*.

TYPOGRAPHER A professional designer of type, books, magazines, and other printed, designed, or digitally published materials.

TYPOGRAPHIC ATTRIBUTES Includes, typeface, size, weight, proportion, slant, style, kerning, leading, wordspace, letterspace, and color.

TYPOGRAPHY The art and craft of creating and/or setting type professionally.

UNCIALS A rounded manuscript style used in the third century in Greece.

UNDERSET (1) A loosely typeset line with excessive word space values. See also: *river*. (2) A line of type not filling a desired measure.

UNIT SET A term used to describe type characters in terms of unit dimensions instead of points.

UNJUSTIFIED TEXT See *flush left; justification; quad left*.

UPPERCASE The capitalized letters of the alphabet and other symbols produced when the SHIFT key on a typewriter-style keyboard is depressed. Originally called uppercase because the lead type version was located in the upper portion of the printer's type case. See also: *lowercase*.

VERSO The reverse, back, or left-hand side of a page, folded sheet, book, or cover. See also: *recto*.

VISUAL COMMUNICATION Also referred to as graphic design, and can be broken down into three categories: (1) information (information/function-based complex graphics), (2) persuasion (product/advertising graphics), and (3) aesthetics (general graphic design pieces, e.g., logos, business cards, brochures).

VISUAL LANGUAGE A set or subset of visual signs by which information can be communicated from one person to another person. These signs are often of a global nature, that is, they can be understood universally, being organized in a preestablished and specified system of symbols. For example, the characters (letters) of an alphabet or any other specified system of symbols or characters. Further elements that affect visual language are page characteristics and composition, typographic attributes, symbolism, color, texture, and other graphic images or elements.

WEIGHT, CHARACTER A typographic term used to specify the variation of a letterform. Weight designations include light, medium, bold, extra bold, and ultra bold.

WIDOW (1) Any objectionably short line at the end of a paragraph or headline. It may be expressed as anything less than four characters, less than a full word, less than a certain percentage of the line measure, or any other subjective definition. (2) Any single line on the top of a page. See also: *orphan*.

WOOD TYPE Blocks of wood into which type characters have been carved in relief. The sizes of wood type were specified in multiples of the pica, and were thus named 8-line, 10-line, etc. Use of wood type predates use of hot-metal composition.

WORD SPACING The amount of spacing between words.

X-HEIGHT A term used to describe the body height of a type character. It is expressed as the total character height without ascenders or descenders. The letters x and z from each typeface are selected to serve as examples of the face body height because they rest on the baseline and vary less in height than curved letters. Alternative term: *z-height*.

X-LINE The line that marks the tops of lowercase letters without ascenders. Alternative term: *mean line*.

Z-HEIGHT. See *x-height*

BIBLIOGRAPHY

Adams, Debra, and Jacques Andres. *New Trends in Digital Typography*. Cambridge, UK: Cambridge University Press, 1989.

Baecker, Ronald M., Aaron Marcus, Ilona R. Posner, et al. *Human Factors and Typography for More Readable Programs*. Reading, MA: Addison-Wesley, 1990.

Baird, Russel N., Duncan McDonald, Ronald K. Pittman, and Arthur T. Turnbull. *The Graphics of Communication: Methods, Media, and Technology*. 6th Ed. Orlando, FL: Holt, Rinehart, and Winston, Inc., 1993.

Bauermeister, Benjamin. *A Manual of Comparative Typography: The PANOSE System*. New York: Van Nostrand Reinhold, 1988.

Bergsland, David. *Printing in a Digital World*. London: Delmar Publishers, Inc., 1997.

Bigelow, Charles, Paul Hayden Duensign, and Linnea Gentry, eds. *Fine Print on Type: The Best Fine Print Magazine on Type and Typography*. San Francisco: Bedford Arts, 1988.

Bringhurst, Robert. *The Elements of Typographic Style*. 1st Ed. Point Roberts: WA: Hartley & Marks, 1992.

Brockmann, Josef Muller. *Grid Systems in Graphic Design*. Heiden, Switzerland: Arthur Niggli Ltd., 1988.

Brockmann, Josef Muller. *Pioneer of Swiss Graphic Design*. Zurich: Lars Muller, 1995.

Carter, Rob, Ben Day, and Phillip Meggs. *Typographic Design: Form and Communication*. New York: Van Nostrand Reinhold Company, 1985.

Clair, Kate. *Typographic: A Primer to History, Techniques, and Artistry*. New York: John Wiley & Sons, Inc., 1993.

Conover, Theodore E. *Graphic Communications Today*. 3d Ed. Reno: West Publishing Company, 1995.

Cook, Alton, and Robert Fleury. *Type and Color*. Rockport, MA: Rockport Publishers, 1989.

Craig, James. *Designing with Type*. New York: Watson-Guptill Publications, 1978.

Dair, Carl. *Design with Type*. Toronto: University of Toronto Press, 1967.

Devall, Sandra Lentz. *Desktop Publishing Guide*. New York: Delmar Publishers, Inc., 1999.

Goudy, Frederic W. *The Alphabet and Elements of Lettering.* Dorset Press Berkeley: University of California Press, 1942.

Greenwald, Martin, and John Luttropp. *Graphic Communications: Design through Production.* New York: Delmar Publishers Inc., 1997.

Haley, Allan. *ALPHABET.* New York: Watson-Guptill Publications, 1995.

——. *The ABC's of Type.* London: Lund Humphries, 1990.

——. *Typographic Milestones.* New York: Van Nostrand Reinhold Company, 1992.

Hurlburt, Allen. *Layout: The Design of the Printed Page.* New York: Watson-Guptill Publications, 1977.

——. *The Grid.* New York: Van Nostrand Reinhold Company, 1978.

Kostelnick, Charles, and David D. Roberts. *Designing Visual Language: Strategies for Professional Communications.* Needham Heights, MA: Allyn and Bacon, 1998.

Kowler, Eileen. *Eye Movements and Their Role in the Visual and Cognitive Processes.* Vol. 4. Amsterdam: Elsevier, 1990.

Lawson, Alexander. *Anatomy of Typeface.* London: Hamish Hamilton, 1990.

Lem, Dean Phillip. *Graphics Master.* 5th Ed. Los Angeles: Dean Lem Associates, Inc., 1993.

Lewis, John. *Typography: Design and Practice.* London: Barrie and Jenkins, 1978.

Lieberman, J. Ben. *Types of Typefaces and How to Recognize Them.* New York: Sterling Publishing Co., 1967.

——. *Type and Typefaces.* New Rochelle, NY: The Myriad Press, 1978.

McLean, Ruari, and Goldine. *Jan Tschichold, Typographer.* London: Lund Humphries, 1975.

Morris, Robert A., Karl Berry, Kathryn A. Hargreaves, and Dimitrios Liarokapis. *How Typeface Variation and Typographic Variation Affect Readability at Small Sizes.* Portland, OR: IS & T's Seventh International Congress on Advances in Non-Impact Printing Technologies, 1991.

Parker, Roger C. *Looking Good in Print.* 4th Ed. Scottsdale, AZ: The Coridis Group, LLC., 1998.

Prust, Z.A. *Graphic Communications: The Printed Image.* Tinley Park, IL: The Goodheart-Willcox Company, Inc., 1999.

Rayner, Keith, ed. *Eye Movements in Reading: Perceptual and Language Processes.* New York: Academic Press, 1983.

——. *The Psychology of Reading.* Englewood Cliffs, NJ: Prentice Hall, 1989.

Romano, Frank J., and Richard M. Romano. *The GATF Encyclopedia of Graphic Communications*. Pittsburgh: GATF*Press*, 1998.

Ryder, John. *The Case for Legibility*. New York: Moretus Press, 1979.

Sierbert, Lori, and Mary Cropper. *Working with Words and Pictures*. Cincinnati, OH: North Lights Books, 1993.

Solomon, Martin. *The Art of Typography*. 2nd Ed. New York: Art Direction Book Company, 1994.

Spencer, Herbert. *Pioneers of Modern Typography*. Cambridge: MIT Press, 1983.

Spiekermann, Erik, and E.M. Ginger. *Stop Stealing Sheep & Find Out How Type Works*. Mountain View, CA: Adobe Press, 1993.

Swann, Alan. *How to Understand and Use Design and Layout*. Cincinnati, OH: North Lights Books, 1987.

Tinker, Miles A. *Legibility of Print*. Ames, IA: Iowa State University Press, 1963.

Tschichold, Jan. *Treasury of Alphabets and Lettering*. Cambridge, MA: Harvard University Press, 1937.

——. *Treasury of Alphabets and Lettering*. New York: Reinhold Publishing Corporation, 1966.

Walker, John R. *Graphic Arts Fundamentals*. Tinley Park, IL: The Goodheart-Willcox Company, Inc., 1992.

Wallis, Lawrence W., ed. *Modern Encyclopedia of Typefaces*. New York: Van Nostrand Reinhold Company, 1990.

Wallschaeger, Charles, and Cynthia Busic-Snyder. *Basic Visual Concepts and Principles for Artists, Architects, and Designers*. Dubuque, IA: Wm. C. Brown Publishers, 1992.

White, Jan V. *Graphic Design for the Electronic Age*. New York: Watson-Guptill Publications, 1988.

Williams, Robin. *The Non-Designer's Design Book*. Berkeley, CA: Peachpit Press, 1994.

——. *The Non-Designer's Type Book*. Berkeley, CA: Peachpit Press, 1998.

Zarchrisson, Bror. *Studies in the Legibility of Printed Text*. Stockholm: Almqvist & Wiksell, 1965.

About the Author

Anthony Faiola is an assistant professor in the Department of Computer Graphics in the area of Interactive Media Development in the School of Technology at Purdue University. He hold three master's degrees: From The Ohio State University he holds a master of arts in Visual Communication & Computer Graphics and a master of fine Arts in Experimental Media, and from SUNY at Albany he holds a master of arts in Printmaking (Lithography). He is a recent recipient of a Fulbright Scholarship to Saint Petersburg, Russia, where he gave a series of lectures on visual communication, graphic user interface design, and digital printing/publishing systems.

He has twenty-five years of professional and academic experience as an art director, teacher, and consultant in visual communication, multimedia, and graphics technology, working with both small and Fortune 500 companies. His designs have been reproduced in various graphic journals and used for more than one hundred publications in the U.S. and abroad. He also has written a series of articles on the subjects of visual communication.

About GATF

The Graphic Arts Technical Foundation is a nonprofit, scientific, technical, and educational organization dedicated to the advancement of the graphic communications industries worldwide. Its mission is to serve the field as the leading resource for technical information and services through research and education. GATF is a partner of the Printing Industries of America (PIA), the world's largest graphic arts trade association, and its regional affiliates.

For 76 years the Foundation has developed leading edge technologies and practices for printing. GATF's staff of researchers, educators, and technical specialists partner with nearly 14,000 corporate members in over 80 countries to help them maintain their competitive edge by increasing productivity, print quality, process control, and environmental compliance, and by implementing new techniques and technologies. Through conferences, satellite symposia, workshops, consulting, technical support, laboratory services, and publications, GATF strives to advance a global graphic communications community.

The Foundation publishes books on nearly every aspect of the field; learning modules (step-by-step instruction booklets); audiovisuals (CD-ROMs and videocassettes); and research and technology reports. It also publishes *GATFWorld*, a bimonthly magazine of technical articles, industry news, and reviews of specific products.

For detailed information about GATF products and services, please visit our website at *http://www.gatf.org* or write to us at 200 Deer Run Road, Sewickley, PA 15143-2600. Phone: 412/741-6860. GATF and PIA publications may also be ordered online through the Graphic Arts Information Network at *http://www.gain.net*.

ABOUT PIA

In continuous operation since 1887 and headquartered in Alexandria, Virginia, Printing Industries of America, Inc. (PIA), is the world's largest graphic art trade association representing an industry with more than 1 million employees and $156 billion in sales annually. PIA promotes the interests of over 14,000 member companies. Companies become members in PIA by joining one of 31 regional affiliate organizations throughout the United States or by joining the Canadian Printing Industries Association. International companies outside North America may join PIA directly.

Printing Industries of America, Inc. is in the business of promoting programs, services, and an environment that helps its members operate profitably. Many of PIA's members are commercial printers, allied graphic arts firms such as electronic imaging companies, equipment manufacturers, and suppliers.

PIA has developed several special industry groups to meet the unique needs of specific market segments. Each special industry group provides members with current information on their specific market and helps members stay ahead of the competition. PIA's special industry groups are the Graphic Communications Association (GCA), Web Offset Association (WOA), Web Printing Association (WPA), Graphic Arts Marketing Information Service (GAMIS), International Thermographers Association (ITA), Label Printing Industries of America (LPIA), and Binding Industries of America International (BIA).

For more detailed information on PIA products and services, please visit our website *http://www.gain.org* or write to 100 Daingerfield Road, Alexandria, VA 22314 (phone: 703/519-8100).

GATF*Press*: Selected Titles

- **Practical Proofreading**
  by Matthew Willen

- **Printing Estimating Primer**
  Don Merit

- **Glossary of Graphic Communications**
  compiled by Pamela Groff

- **Understanding Graphic Communication**
  by Harvey Robert Levenson, Ph.D.

- **Handbook of Printing Processes**
  by Deborah Stevenson

- **Flexography Primer**
  by J. Page Crouch

- **Gravure Primer**
  by Cheryl Kasunich

- **Lithography Primer**
  by Dan Wilson

- **On-Demand & Digital Printing Primer**
  by Howard M. Fenton

- **The GATF Encyclopedia of Graphic Communications**
  by Frank Romano and Richard Romano

- **Handbook of Graphic Arts Equations**
  by Manfred H. Breede

- **Screen Printing Primer**
  by Samuel Ingram

Colophon

This first edition of *Typography Primer* was edited, designed and printed at the Graphic Arts Technical Foundation, headquartered in Sewickley, Pennsylvania. The text was created by the author using Microsoft Word, then edited at GATF and imported into QuarkXPress 4.0 on an Apple Power Macintosh. The primary fonts used for the interior of the book are New Baskerville and Futura. Illustrations are in TIFF, JPEG, and EPS formats and were adjusted using Adobe Illustrator 8.0.1 and Adobe Photoshop 5.5. Pages were proofed on a Xerox Regal color copier with Splash RIP.

Once the editorial/page layout process was completed, the images were transmitted to GATF's Center for Imaging Excellence, where all images were adjusted for the printing parameters of GATF's in-house printing department and proofed.

Next, the entire book was preflighted, digitally imposed using DK&A INposition, and then output to a Barco Crescent 42 plate-setter. The interior of the book was printed as 16- and 32-page signatures on GATF's 26×40-in., four-color Heidelberg Speedmaster Model 102-4P sheetfed perfecting press and the cover was printed four-up on GATF's 20×28-in., six-color Komori Lithrone 28 sheetfed press with tower coater. Finally, the book was sent to a trade bindery for perfect binding.